SELF-COMPASSION & DIALECTICAL BEHAVIOR THERAPY

Discover The Secret To Self Compassion and Love Through The Power of DBT To Bring Happiness, Joy, Success, and Peace in Your Life

Lawrence McDonagh PsyD

Dr. Edmund Gazipurg
Brene Engel PsyD
Dr. Barry Brown M.D.
Dr. Christopher Beverly M.D

Table of Contents

Introduction 3

PART 1 4

Chapter 1- What is Self Compassion 5

Chapter 2- Benefits of Self-Compassion 10

Chapter 3- Myths about Self Compassion 16

Chapter 4- Dealing with Negativity 25

Chapter 5- Building and Mastering Emotions 40

Chapter 6- Practical Steps for Becoming Self Compassionate 48

PART 2 67

Chapter 1: Is This for You? 69

Chapter 2: Your Toolbox, DBT 71

Chapter 3: Finding Yourself through Mindfulness 76

Chapter 4: Taking Mindfulness to the Next Level with Advanced Meditation Techniques 80

Chapter 5: Using Your New Tools to Process Negative Emotions 85

Chapter 6: Defining Your Goals, Your Values, and Yourself 90

Chapter 8: How DBT Has Enhanced Your Life 97

Conclusion 102

Introduction

Do you constantly find yourself doubting your own capabilities, being hard on yourself, always thinking you are not good enough? In this book, you will be introduced to self-compassion, what it is and what it isn't, the myths surrounding self-compassion and why it is worth introducing self-compassion in your life.

Reading and journeying through all the different chapters in this book, you will come to realize that it is about encouraging you to give self-compassion a try especially if you find yourself having negative thoughts and not giving yourself a break. It is easy to think that we are not good enough or we are not doing our best simply because we live in a culture of endless competition and striving and at times like this, self-compassion may seem like a luxury that none of us can afford but in truth, we can.

As a matter of fact, it is a luxury we cannot afford to live without. We need it because it helps us become better human beings to ourselves personally and to the people around us. In this book, you will see the different research that has been conducted showing how self-compassion ultimately leads us to life healthy lives, cultivate good habits, lower our depression and anxiety as well as have more satisfying relationships.

By cultivating self-compassion, you will be in a better position of assessing and acknowledging the challenges you are experiencing and develop more wise, thoughtful and helpful ways to respond. Self-compassion promotes understanding and acceptance on a personal and interpersonal level, in a way that encourages and empowers you to make positive change. By the end of this book, hopefully you have gathered enough information to help you be more self-compassionate and practice the necessary exercises to help promote self-compassionate in every aspect of your life.

PART 1

Chapter 1- What is Self Compassion

What is the self-compassion? Have you thought about it or experienced it from someone?

The truth is, having compassion for yourself is not different from having compassion for other people or animals. Having self-compassion is being kind to yourself and understanding to your needs when you face personal failures. Think about how you would talk and console a friend who's going through a rough time- what would you say to them? Would you be harsh to them? Would you say things that bring them down even more?

The answers to those questions are of course a big NO. You would do what all good friends do- bring them up when they feel down, hug them and tell them everything is going to be ok, telling them that you'll be there for them to talk to or if they need help. Self-compassion is acting this same way towards yourself when you go through a rough patch. You notice the suffering and you empathize with yourself by comforting yourself, offering kindness and understanding.

Kristin D. Neff and Katie A. Dahm are two prominent are two names synonymous with the research on self-compassion. In their book, the Handbook of Mindfulness and Self-Regulation, it states that there are three primary components to self-compassion:

1. Self-kindness
2. Common humanity
3. Mindfulness

To understand self compassion, we need to consider what it means to feel compassion on a general level. Here are some views of compassion:

- The Buddhist point of view of compassion is given to our own as well as to others suffering.
- Goetz, Keltner & Simon- Thomans, 2010: Compassion is the sensitivity to the suffering that is happening, coupled with a deep desire to alleviate that suffering
- Neff, 2003a: Self-compassion is compassion directed inwards, referring to ourselves as the object of concern and care when we are faced with an experience of suffering

The Three Elements of Self-Compassion

The key to understanding self-compassion is to understand the difference between this trait and more negative ones. Sometimes when we give ourselves self-compassion, it may be construed as narcissism to a point, which is why it is important to know what is self-compassion and to what degree is it considered self-compassion and when it isn't.

1. Self-kindness is not Self-Judgement

Self-compassion is being understanding and warm to ourselves when we fail, or when we suffer or at moments when we feel inadequate. We should not be ignoring these emotions or criticizing yourself. People who have self-compassion understand that being human comes with its own imperfections and failing is part of the human experience. It is inevitable that there will be no failure when we attempt something because failure is part of learning and progress. We will look into how failure is a friend in disguise in the next chapters. Having self-compassion is also being gentle with yourself when faced with painful experiences rather than getting angry at everything and anything that falls short of your goals and ideals.

Things cannot be exactly the way it should be or supposed to be or how we dream it to be. There will be changes and when we accept this with kindness and sympathy and understanding, we experience greater emotional equanimity.

2. Common humanity and not Isolation

It is a common human emotion to feel frustrated especially when things do not go the way we envision them to be. When this happens, frustration is usually accompanied by irrational isolation, making us feel and think that we are the only person on earth going through this or making dumb mistakes like this. News flash- all humans suffer, all of us go through different kinds of suffering at varying degrees. Self-compassion involves recognizing that we all suffer and all of us have personal inadequacies. It does not happen to 'Me' or 'I' alone.

3. Mindfulness is not Over-Identification

Self-compassion needs us to be balanced with our approach so that our negative emotions are neither exaggerated or suppressed. This balance act comes out from the process of relating our personal experiences with that of the suffering of others. This puts the situation we are going through into a larger perspective.

We need to keep mindful awareness so that we can observe our own negative thoughts and emotions with clarity and openness. Having a mindful approach is non-judgemental and it is a state of mindful reception that enables us to observe our feelings and thoughts without denying them or suppressing them. There is no way that we can ignore our pain and feel compassion at the same time. By having mindfulness, we also prevent over-identification of our thoughts and feelings.

Discovering Self Compassion

You're so dumb! You don't belong here loser! Those jeans make you look like a fat cow! You can't sit with us! It's safe to say we've all heard some kind rude, unwanted comments either directly or indirectly aimed at us. Would you talk like this to a friend? Again, the answer is a big NO.

Believe it or not, it is a lot easier and natural for us to be kind and nice to people than to be mean and rude to them whether it is a stranger or someone we care about in our lives. When someone we care is hurt or is going through a rough time, we console them and say it is ok to fail. We support them when they feel bad about themselves and we comfort them to make them feel better or just to give a shoulder to cry on.

We are all good at being understanding and compassionate and kind to others. How often do we offer this same kindness and compassion to ourselves? Research on self-compassion shows that those who are compassionate are less likely to be anxious, depressed or stressed and more resilient, happy and optimistic. In other words, they have better mental health.

Conclusion

It does make sense that people who have better self-compassion are happier and optimistic about their future. When we continuously criticise ourselves and berate ourselves, we end up feeling incompetent, worthless and insecure. This cycle of negativity continue to self-sabotage us and sometimes, we end up self harming ourselves.

But when our positive inner voice triumphs and plays the role of the supportive friend, we create a sense of safety and we accept ourselves enough to see a better and clear vision. We then work towards making the required changes for us to be healthier and happier. But if we do not do this, we are working ourselves towards a downward spiral or chaos, unhappiness and stress.

In the next chapters, we will look into the benefits of self-compassion, self-esteem, how to get rid of negative self-talk, mastering our emotions as well as practical exercises towards becoming self-compassionate.

Chapter 2- Benefits of Self-Compassion

You've probably heard your parents say time and time again to treat others as you would want them to treat you. Therefore, we are often taught to be empathetic and compassionate to others who are facing difficulties and challenges in their life. However, when faced with our own personnel challenges be it in our everyday lives, work and relationships, we often find ourselves becoming our own worst enemy. Hence we become too critical and judgmental on our own selves and in turn prevent any healing process from taking place.

Therefore, instead of being self-critical to oneself, we need to develop the concept of self-compassion in combating our negative thoughts and self-criticism that keeps us from overcoming our obstacles and challenges.

Self-compassion is defined as being compassionate to our own suffering, inadequacies, weakness and failures. As we know from the previous chapter, Kristin Neff, an associate professor at department of educational psychology in the University of Texas further breaks down self-compassion to 3 key elements which are self-kindness, common humanity and mindfulness.

Self-kindness is about recognizing our flaws and issues as well as being caring to oneself when going through bouts of hardship and challenges. Common humanity on the other hand, puts emphasis that the suffering and anguish we go through is all a natural part of being human and it's a normal part of everyday life. Lastly, mindfulness deals with the individual's ability to take a middle path in addressing their sufferings so as not to neglect or overthinking the situation.

Various research done on the topic of self-compassion indicates that individuals who practice self-compassion have a far greater psychological health than those who lack it. The individuals who practice self-compassion have a more positive life satisfaction, happiness and optimism. Apart from that self-compassion is also connected low levels of anxiety, self-criticism and depression. As such, in a way self-compassion can be used as a tool to develop inner strength when facing challenges in every aspect of our life.

So we know what self-compassion is and sure it helps us lead a better life and have better relationships. What other aspects of self-compassion are there? Here are some major benefits you can reap from being self-compassion. We explore it in terms of work, relationships and in life.

Self-Compassion At Work

Our daily work environment can be a long-lasting love-hate relationship with its own ups and downs that one has to face on a daily basis. As such, we are constantly bombarded with undue stress in meeting deadlines, reports and customer expectations. Many at times, we will face moments that completely overwhelm us and have a negative impact on us. This can be caused by numerous factors such as a negative remark by a colleague, superior or even a customer, failure to reach sales targets or goals, not getting that raise or promotion that you so deserve or even by making an unintentional mistake at the job. Since we all strive to achieve more and be perfect at our jobs, this negative circumstances will have an adverse effect if not dealt properly and swiftly.

Self-compassion can be used at work through the following means to reap various benefits: -

- Conducting a post-mortem to review the shortcomings and failures of a certain project or task and learning from these failures to prevent similar occurrences in the future.
- When facing criticism and rejection from colleagues, superiors and customers, instead of being self-critical and falling into complete despair, we will be able to be calm and focus our energies and thoughts of improving ourselves and not to allow stress to overwhelm ourselves.
- Applying self-compassion at work also helps us in being resilient through difficult scenarios especially is situations that we don't get a certain reward or promotion that we think we deserve.
- Self-compassion enables us to be more creative. When we fail a project or we do not complete a task or when a work event doesn't go as expected, being self-compassionate to ourselves will help us to look back at the series of events and instead of berating ourselves, we look back and see what we could have done better and learn from our mistakes. It makes us becoming more creative the next time around.
- Self-compassion builds trust. It enables you to be transparent and authentic, makes it easier for people to connect with you because you are your true self.

- Showing genuine compassion to yourself also means showing compassion to the people around you. When you show compassion to yourself, you extend this feeling to your co-workers and it makes them feel safe.
- Self compassion allows you to allow yourself and your team implicit permission to do their very best without worry of punishment or repercussions if something doesn't go right.

Self-Compassion In Relationships

In the topic of relationships be it a romantic or non-romantic relationship, we often find ourselves in situations of disagreement from time to time. And these can sometimes lead to moments of stress and unhappiness between oneself and their significant other/parent/sibling/friend. Self-compassion provides various ways much like our situations at work to help us deal with this issues and challenges. Many studies done on this matter point that self-compassion when used have the following positive impact on relationships: -

- Individuals who practice self-compassion know that every individual as well as themselves aren't perfect and are subjected to weaknesses and shortcomings
- They are able relate to their partners much better
- They are more warm and compassionate in understanding a situation
- They are more open to compromising to resolve a situation
- Individuals who are self-compassionate have better empathy. The bring out the best in their partners.

- They are more responsive and aware to the issues that their partner faces
- They are better listeners, they listen to understand and not answer
- People who practice self-compassion own up to their mistakes

Studies also have shown that individuals that lack self-compassion tend to have a negative effect on people around them which may lead to isolation. As such, those people who practice self-compassion have healthier and happier relationships and have a bigger a wide social circle.

Self-Compassion In Life

When encountering difficulties in daily life which can range from a number of issues/aspects such as health to financial issues, we need to act by being compassionate and kind to ourselves. When faced with various issues on a daily basis, self-compassion allows us to look for solutions to take care of oneself instead of berating or being overly critical of one's lack of accomplishments or weaknesses.

With that being said, an individual who practices self-compassion will look into various ways to engage their mind and body into healthy activities that can stimulate them and lets them focus on positive aspects instead of groveling on a negative situation. This can be in a form of an exercise, a hobby, prayer or even a warm bath or a cup of tea to calm themselves down.

Self-compassionate individuals tend to be more: -

- Happier
- Satisfied with life

- Resilient
- Emotionally intelligent
- Have better coping mechanisms
- Optimistic
- Creative
- Less judgemental
- Better goal-getters
- It greatly reduces mental problems

As such, cultivating the habits of self-compassion in every aspect of our life will allow to become the best version of ourselves and allow us to live much happier with the right mindset.

Chapter 3- Myths about Self Compassion

Many people do not have any issues with showing compassion to other people- it is a commendable quality. Compassion is often seen with kindness, tenderness, understanding, sympathy, empathy and of course the impulse to help those in need, whether human or animal.

However, with self-compassion, that is a different story altogether. For plenty of people, having self-compassion often relates to negative qualities such as self-serving, self-pity, self-centered, indulgent and just selfish. We seem to think that if we are not hard on ourselves or punishing ourselves over our failures and flaws, we risk a runaway ego and fall into the traps of false pride.

Take for example, Norman. A young bank executive who is also a new father. Between juggling work and a new baby, he also spends time volunteering as a football coach at a local shelter. He is a committed father and husband, a hard worker and a community role-model. But Norman has gone through several episodes of anxiety attacks simply because he feels overwhelmed, he feels he isn't contributing enough in his team at work and isn't good enough as a husband or father.

People have misgivings about self-compassion and it is only because nobody really knows what it looks like, or even how to practice it so it doesn't become excessive and borderline narcissistic. Self compassion has the element of mindfulness, of wisdom and the recognition to common humanity. Research by Kristin Neff points the myths that people have on self-compassion is the main reason why most of us are in the cycle of criticizing yourself over and over again. Here are the common myths:

#1 Self-Compassion is just a person crying out for self-pity

Let's get this straight- self compassion does not mean you are feeling sorry for yourself. It is fact an antidote to self-pity. It isn't about whining about our bad luck but instead, self-compassion makes us more open to acknowledging, accepting and experiencing difficult feelings with the help of kindness. Self-compassionate people have a lower tendency of wallowing in self-pity about how bad the circumstances may be and this leads to better mental clarity and mental health.

Filip Raes of the University of Leuven conducted a study on the connection between self-compassion, mental health and ruminative thinking. This study was conducted among the students in his university. Students were first assessed using the Self-Compassion Scale developed by Dr. Kristin Neff. Participants were asked how often they responded to behaviors that corresponded with the main components of self-compassion. These behaviors included "I try to be patient and understanding towards the elements of my personality that I am not fond of"; "When things are going badly for me, I see them as part of life that happens to everyone".

The result of the study showed that students who had better self-compassion parameters were less whiny and broody when things did not go their way. They were also less anxious and less depressed and showed better signs of attentiveness.

#2 Self-compassion is a sign of weakness

Melissa, as a first born child was always seen as the responsible one, a label she has taken on with pride. She sees herself as a pillar of strength to her family. However, since Melissa got married, she has decided to take a step back and pay more attention to her new marriage. While her own family has never imposed on her, Melissa secretly feels as if she is not being a good daughter, and racked with guilt. When her friends suggested that she try not being too hard on herself, her reaction was to immediately tell them off, saying that self-compassion does not make her a good daughter. What Melissa does not know is that this is not a sign of her abandoning her family or a sign of weakness but discovering self-compassion is part of the process of resilience to us. When going through changes in life, self-compassion enables us to survive and thrive.

#3 Self-Compassion can make you a complacent person

Thinking that self-compassion makes you complacent is one of the biggest blocks you can place on yourself. It's so easy for us to criticize ourselves just because we fail to live up to certain standards and we immediately label ourselves as sloths. Do we do this to our kids too?

Amanda's daughter just failed her Biology test and upon finding out, Amanda starts berating her, saying that she is stupid and that she is ashamed of her. This is the exact same thing that Amanda tells herself when she fails to live up to a certain expectation. Rather than motivating her daughter, these comments on her daughter lose faith in herself and prevents her from trying to do better.

What Amanda can do however is practice a more compassionate approach to the situation by giving a hug, telling her daughter that it happens to anyone and what support can she give her daughter. Telling her daughter that she believes in her will help motivate her.

Amanda needs to give honest recognition to the failure as well as empathize with her daughter's unhappiness. This caring response helps us boost out self-confidence and spread emotional support.

While Amanda may not have said those words to her daughter, she still believes deep down that this type of negative feedback may spur her daughter to achieve the necessary goals. But thanks research on human emotions and its responses, showing self-compassion is more effective to boost a better rate of success than self-punishment.

Juliana Breines and Serena Chen of University of California conducted a research to examine the effects of self-compassion and to see how or if it was one of the factors that motivated participants to get involved in positive behaviors and make positive changes. Participants were ask to think back at a time when they felt guilty about such as lying to a partner, cheating in an exam which made them feel bad even till now. They were then randomly assigned to write to themselves from three different perspectives:

1. that of a compassionate and understanding friend
2. write about their own positive qualities
3. write about a hobby they enjoyed doing

Researchers found that participants involved in the self-compassionate perspective were more remorseful for their wrong doing and were more motivated to not repeat the offence.

The research concluded that self-compassion was not about evading personal accountability, rather strengthening it. Acknowledging our failures with kindness rather than judgements enables us to see ourselves clearly beyond the spectacles of self-judgement. Tell ourselves 'I can't believe I messed up. I got so stressed and I overreacted' rather than 'I cannot believe i said that. Why am I so mean?'

#4 Self-Compassions makes us more narcissistic

To many Americans, having high self-esteem means that you are special and beyond average. For some people with high self-esteem, the minute that we receive a less than average score, our self-esteem crashes and plummets. There is no way that everyone to be above average all the time. There are some areas that we can excel because we are naturally good at it but then there are aspects that we either under perform or we are just average. That is why diversity is good. At times when we do perform below average, we see ourselves like failures. The desire to be above average is always going to be there, as we like that feeling of high self-esteem. However this can make us be develop nasty behaviors.

Jean Twenge, a researcher from the San Diego University and Keith Campbell from the University of Georgia have been studying narcissism scores since 1987 among college students. It may not come as a surprise to you to know that among modern-day social media savvy students, narcissism ran high.

It is extremely important to note the difference between self-compassion and self-esteem. While they are both connected to our psychological well-being, the difference is very vivid:

- Self-esteem is evaluating your self-worth positively
- Self-compassion is relating to the changes that happen to us with kindness and acceptance

With self-esteem, we want to feel better than the people around us but with self-compassion, we acknowledge the fact that we have and share certain imperfections. Self-esteem is buoyancy, depending on our latest success or failure. Those with higher levels of self-esteem tend to get upset when they receive neutral feedback. They often start thinking 'Am I just average? I thought i was exceptional'. They are also likelier to listen to any feedback that is related to their personality and blame it on external factors. Self-esteem thrives only when the reviews are good which leads to evasiveness.

Self-compassionate people on the other hand are more emotionally stable despite the degree of praise they receive.

#5 Self-compassion makes us selfish

It is easy to conflate self-compassion with selfishness. Joshua for example spends a large portion of his day caring for his family and at weekends, he supports activities at the local college. He was raised in a family placed importance on service to others. This eventually led him to think that spending time for self-care and being kind and caring to his needs meant he must be neglecting the people around him just for his own needs.

There are plenty of people like Joshua- selfless, good, altruistic and generous to others but horrible to their own selves. When we become too absorbed in self-judgement, we end up giving less because we are preoccupied by thinking about our inadequacies and worthless selves.

Plenty of our emotional needs are met when we are kind and nurturing to ourselves which leaves us in a better position to focus on the people around us. However, caring for the welfare of others often becomes a bigger priority and the idea of treating ourselves badly starts rearing its ugly head. Think about the safety message on an airplane. It is advised to place the oxygen mask over your ownself before assisting others right? This is the same for self compassion.

Kristin Neff conducted a research with Tasha Beretvas of the University of Texas just to prove that being good to ourselves is more helpful when we want to be good to others. The research look at whether people who were self-compassionate were more giving in their relationships. It explored 100 couple who are in romantic relationships for a year or longer. Participants were asked to rate themselves based on the Self-Compassion Scale.

Neff & Beretvas found that partners who were self-compassionate individuals were described as more accepting, caring and supportive compared to self-critical partners who were seen as detached, controlling and aggressive. Self-compassionate partners brought to the table a more secure and satisfied relationship.

A growing research also focuses on therapists and caregivers who were more self-compassionate. Those who were were less likely to feel caregiver burnout and they were more satisfied with their careers, they were more happy, they felt more energized and were more grateful to be able to make a difference.

Conclusion

Self-compassion enables us to feel love, courage, wisdom and generosity in a more sustainable way. It gives us a boundless and directionless mental and emotional state. The power of self-compassion can be enriched through practice and of course through learning, just like so many other good habits.

Being kind to ourselves is not a selfish luxury or a sign of weakness or self-pity. It is a gift to our persons to make us happier and more fulfilled. Thanks to the many research conducted, we now know the myths of self-compassion.

Chapter 4- Dealing with Negativity

Did you ever realize that it is much easier to be happy than it is to be unhappy? Go ahead. Think about it. While you are reading this, just think about the many things that happened before you opening this book and reading. What happened when you woke up? Did you get a kiss from your partner? How did your coffee taste this morning? How is the weather outside like now? All these things that happened to you today, what made you happy and what made you sad?

If you listed ten things today and 7 of them were things that made your happy and three made you unhappy, sad, frustrated or moody, then most likely you were grateful, and you were positive. The thing is, many of us would prefer to be happy and positive rather than be unhappy and negative. And it is that simple to be positive and happy. Also, positive thinking is above and beyond just being happy or displaying a cheerful and upbeat attitude. It also creates and establishes value in your life and relationships, and it also helps you build skills that benefit you longer than your smile can take you. Barbara Fredrickson, a positive psychology researcher from the University of North Carolina, published a landmark paper on the impact of positive thinking on work, health and general wellbeing. Here's a little brief of Barbara's research:

What Can Negative Thinking do to your Brain?

Our brain is programmed to respond to negative emotions by shutting off the world around us and limiting the options we see around us. For example, if you get into a fight with your sister, your emotions and anger might consume to the point where you react adversely- you can't think about anything else. Or for instance your coffee this morning spilled on your shirt, and this creates a domino effect of everything going wrong in your day, and you get so stressed out that you find it hard to start or do anything because you've lost your focus. Or if you are supposed to complete a project but you didn't, you start to feel bad about it and all you think is how irresponsible you are and that you are lazy, and you lack motivation. The point is, our brain shuts off from the outside world and relies on the negative emotions of fear, stress, and anger. Negative thoughts and emotions prevent us from seeing other options, solutions or choices that are around us.

What Can Positive Thinking do to your Brain?

Barbara Fredrickson also explains how positive thinking manifests in our brain. She explains with an experiment where research subjects are divided into five groups, and each group is shown a different video clip. The first group was shown clips that created feelings of joy whereas the second group was shown clips that created contentment, the third was the control group that had images of no significant emotions and were neutral whereas group four had clips that created fear and group five had clips that created the feelings of anger.

Participants were then asked to imagine themselves in situations that these same emotions would come about and write down their reactions to it. Participants that viewed images of fear and anger had the least responses or reactions whereas participants who saw joy and contentment had more reactions. The bottom line is, if you experience positive emotions you will see more possibilities in life. Positive emotions broaden our possibilities and thinking, thus opening up more options for us in facing issues, crisis, problems, and solutions and so on. In the next few chapters, we will discuss how we can work our mind to be more positive and look at things in a more positive perspective to enhance and give more value to our life, relationships, and goals. It is not as hard as it seems because all it takes is a little practice.

Have you seen the movie Inside Out?

If you did, then you will probably realize that being sad is a good thing- not always, but this emotion is there for a reason. When we talk about dealing with negativity, it doesn't necessarily mean being optimistic all the time, especially in the face of suffering.

Pain and sadness are just part of the complex human emotions all of us have, and it is just as important to feel pain and sadness, guilt and fear as this are all part and parcel of coping. Experiencing and processing negative emotions in a healthy way is a crucial part of personal growth.

There are two scenarios when people are confronted with negative situations. One, they either obsess over the problem or two, they numb their emotions. Either of these coping methods is not healthy, and it can create harmful patterns in our mind, over a period of time. Obsessing is deceptive because it feels as if you are thinking things through but to continuously obsess over a situation only reinforces the impact of the negative thoughts and emotions.

That said, numbing your emotions towards a pained situation isn't good either because it really is not possible to selectively numb out an emotion. Humans are so complex that our range of emotions does not enable us to directly shut down an emotion. If you somehow blot out anger, you'll blur out happiness and serenity too. Why? Because while you like being active and optimistic all the time, not showing anger to something that has hurt you or pained you or frustrated you, will make you feel more bitter eventually. Only because you weren't able to express your anger, the situation or the person related to this will not know how you feel. For example, if we use alcohol to numb our pain, we do not learn how to cope with sadness. We just develop another problem which is alcohol abuse.

If you are going through a pained time, then you need to develop healthy coping skills, and this involves recognizing the inevitability and necessity of some suffering and moving on from it. The process usually includes:

- Acknowledging your negative feelings and watch them with a non-judgmental attitude
- Recognize when they are triggered and assess your reactions when responding to this
- Understand that pain is just a catalyst for growth and resilience
- Practice forgiveness towards those who have pained you
- Express yourself in creative and healthy ways like painting or exercising
- Seek the support of others

Steps to deal with Negative thoughts and Events

Here are some tried and tested ways to overcome negative thoughts and events which you can try:

1. Meditate or do yoga.

Yoga helps take your focus away from your thoughts and bring attention to your breath. Yoga or meditation is very relaxing, and it helps ease one's mind. It also helps you stay present and focused on the moment that is happening.

2. Smile.

Pain and sadness can make it very hard to smile. While it does seem hard to smile when you aren't feeling so happy inside, you need to sometimes force this out of you. So try doing this in front of a mirror everyday or make a mental note to smile to the people you correspond with daily.

3. Surround yourself with positive people.

Surround yourself with friends and family that can give you constructive and loving feedback. Each time you feel you are going down into your negative spiral, call these people up and speak to them so they can put your focus back again to where it's needed to be at the time.

4. Change your thoughts from negative to positive.

Easier said than done, no doubt but you can turn any situation into a positive one. For example, if you have just started a new job you barely have enough experience of, instead of saying 'I'll take a long time to adjust or learn' just say 'I will take on any challenges because challenges excite me!'

5. Don't wallow in self-pity. Take charge of your life

You are the captain of your shop so do not make yourself a victim. There is always a way out of any situation so if it becomes to unbearable, then leave. Otherwise, you stay put and make the best of it and don't point fingers, blame, complain or whine.

6. Volunteer

Volunteering also takes the focus away. If you think you are in a bad situation, imagine the people who need food aid or money. Do something nice for someone else so volunteer at an organization or donate.

7. Remember to keep moving forward

We easily dwell on our mistakes and feel terrible for the way we acted. But you can't reverse the situation so instead of feeling sorry for yourself or beating yourself up over what you'd done, tell yourself that you'd made a mistake, you learned from it, and you want to move on.

8. Listen to music

One of the best ways to alleviate your mood especially in the morning is by listening to songs and singing in the shower! It doesn't matter if you remember the lyrics – a good happy song will put you in a good and happy mood.

9. Be grateful

Being grateful enables you to appreciate all the things you have. So be grateful every day.

10. Read positive quotes.

Just log into Pinterest, read positive quotes every day. Better yet, print out the ones that you like and stick in on your wall, your fridge or your computer.

Learn to Forgive Yourself

Just like negative emotions, failure is also good to experience because it only makes us stronger.

Yes! Failure is something that didn't kill you. You're still alive! So what doesn't kill you only makes you stronger. Why do you need experience failure? Nobody wants to experience failure but if you looked at the successful people in our generation today, or even the past- they all failed. They all made mistakes. They all went through trial and error. What sets them apart from the perennial failures? They didn't give up. They learnt from their mistakes. They had extreme passion, making them eager to keep on trying till they succeeded. Here's why you need to experience failure:

Without failure, you'd be sucked into a blissful feeling that nothing can go wrong and that everything you'd put into place will work exactly as how it should be

When something does go wrong, you are unable to cope with the change or adapt to create solutions.

Failure enables us to work on our flaws and it also allows us to right our wrongs. Failure also enables us upgrade or enhance or refine our work, technique and solutions

Failure also teaches us a lesson. It is our choice to learn from it or run from it

When we fail, it's easy to get discouraged and upset and we develop a sense of being afraid to fail again. In order to be successful in anything that we do, we just need to remind ourselves to let go of our pride and ego. Failure only makes us grow wiser, make us more adaptable and vivid to any possible scenarios that could happen. We are more prepared to face the same problem but at a different angle.

So how do you look at failure at a positive way? We need to redefine the way we view failure. The fear of failure is what stops many great individuals from creating something beneficial and meaningful in our world. The fear of failure is why we stop ourselves from living extraordinary lives.

The fear of failure is why we never submitted the novel we wrote, we never expressed our feelings to the people we love, never bungee jumped or telling someone how you really feel.

Daniel Epstein, founder of Unreasonable group stresses the point of re-branding the way we see failure. He suggests defining it as such:

"To Fail means "to not start doing something you believe in. To stop doing something you believe in just because it is hard. To ignore your gut instinct around what you believe is right and wrong."

In actual fact, many of the world's greatest philosophers, entrepreneurs, scientists and artisans have all expressed their thoughts on failure and how it has helped them overcome adversity and obstacles. All these perceptions tell us that fear of failure is evident in every human being but with passion and perseverance to achieve what you want will be the driving force in the determination between constant failure and success.

Hopefully, these quotes will give you a good perspective. After all, what better way to learn than to be inspired by some of the most successful people on earth?

Remembering that I'll be dead soon is the most important tool I've ever encountered to help me make the big choices in life. Because almost everything – all external expectations, all pride, all fear of embarrassment or failure – these things just fall away in the face of death, leaving only what is truly important. ~Steve Jobs

I've missed more than 9000 shots in my career. I've lost almost 300 games. 26 times, I've been trusted to take the game winning shot and missed. I've failed over and over and over again in my life. And that is why I succeed. ~Michael Jordan

Our doubts are traitors, and make us lose the good we oft might win, by fearing to attempt. ~William Shakespeare

For every failure, there's an alternative course of action. You just have to find it. When you come to a roadblock, take a detour. ~Mary Kay Ash

Failure is blindness to the strategic element in events; success is readiness for instant action when the opportune moment arrives. ~Newell D. Hillis

The only real failure in life is not to be true to the best one knows. ~Buddha

Success is often achieved by those who don't know that failure is inevitable. ~Coco Chanel

Steps to Overcome Failure

Highly successful people are the ones who have failed the most. We only hear about their successes but never the trials and tribulations and obstacles that they had to go through. Setbacks and failures are part of life and nobody is perfect. Yes we fall into hard times at some point in our lives but what this is all a lesson to us. If we can manage it effectively, then no matter what comes our way in the future, we can overcome it. Here are four steps that can help you turn any negative experience into a positive one:

- **Failure is part of the road to success**

When times get tough, the tough get going. It is frustrating to hear people tell us to be positive when we are faced with adversity but this doesn't mean we have to be smiling all the time or be happy all the time. Staying positive is knowing that despite your setback, you can bounce back again. Staying positive is learning and growing and evolving. Understand that setbacks aren't the end of the road; rather it is carving a step in our journey to succeed. When life hits you with a setback, its okay to be sad and frustrated and upset- but we should never stay down.

- **Blow your Steam off**

When you hit a setback or a failure, your mind gets clouded. You worked so hard to get to this point, only to fail. If you have come to this point, take a step back and evaluate your work. Take some time off to clear your head and accept your mistakes. Once you have done this, you will begin to accept what has happened and how it happened or why it happened. This emotional state will eventually evaporate and then you can go back to focus on the work at hand.

- **Be Honest**

Being brutally honest to ourselves in the midst of a failure is a trait of success. Most people do not want to admit their mistake or admit that it is their own fault that all these negative scenarios have happened. The thing is, part of being positive is also about being responsible and being accountable to ourselves and the mistakes we have made. We need to do this because this is how we learn. Albert Einstein once said that it is crazy to keep doing the same thing over and over again and expecting different results. That is why learning from our mistakes is a crucial part of moving on and part of learning. If we do not learn from our mistakes, we are doomed to be repeating them again and again and again.

- **Move Forward**

We need to move forward each time we fail. When we fail, we fail forward which means learning from our setbacks and then, making the necessary adjustments until we reach success. You have come so far, do not give up. So each change we make, each person we meet and every tiny bit of information we learn all combines to create a different outcome for us to learn from.

Obstacles are inevitable in life but there are always two ways of handling them. While they may block your focus out temporarily, our perseverance is the element that determines whether we fall back or move forward. As we get more and more efficient in the journey of positive thinking, we will enable ourselves to always see the positive side of things even in the most darkest of situations or the hardest of times.

Surrounding yourself with Positive People

No doubt that people have a huge impact on your life. According to Jim Rohn, American entrepreneur and motivation speaker, we all spend our time with an average of five people. With this in mind, think about who these 5 people are and how they impact your life.

Some people, including your friends whom you've known for a long time, can be parasites. These parasites suck out your energy and happiness and even your resources.

So what makes someone a 'good' person you can spend your time with? What are the benefits of surrounding yourself with self-disciplined people?

Your GOOD Category

The people around you can be good in so many ways. This doesn't mean that they go to church every Sunday. It's more like feeding the poor, looking after abandon dogs or something simple like encouraging you to hit the gym more often. These people can be your friends, your family, your co-workers and even some acquaintances.

In essence, good people are productive people. They have a lot of good traits in them that inspire and motivate you too.

It is also important to note too much of something good can also inhibit your growth. You need diversity and healthy arguments and discussions along the way. Always be eager to learn new knowledge and look at different perspectives from your peers.

Think About How You Interact with People

Time for a little exercise. Write down the names of the five people you usually spend time with. Then, write down the qualities you see in them. Think about how they positively or negatively affect you. Are you happy around them? Do they make you feel like you got what it takes to reach your goals? Do they support you? If your list has more positives than negatives, then you probably have the good people around you.

You want to surround yourself with people who make you happy, with those that make you feel alive, the people who help you when you are in need and those that make you feel safe- they are the ones who genuinely care and are worth keeping in your life.

The key here is to finding what is good for you because what is good for you may be different for someone else.

So how do you do that?

Your vibe is what will attract the people around you. When you give off good vibes, good vibes will follow you. You will also feel less stressed and find joy even in the most simplest things like the blue sky or a scoop of vanilla ice cream.

So train your mind to not think negatively and try to see the positive side of things. It is ok to feel sadness and grief and bitterness when things don't go the way you want or something bad happens but if you start building a home in the negativity scene, it'll be harder for you to leave it.

Today, make a commitment to start spending more time with the good people in your life.

Benefits of surrounding yourself with Positive People

1. You Do not get into needless battles

Thoughts become things- you've heard it before. But some of these things are also feelings and feelings are energy. The feelings of happiness, sadness, gratitude, confidence are all energy- negative and positive. When you surround yourself with positive people, you eliminate negative energy, thus eliminate unnecessary conflicts.

You get to live in the feeling of gratitude more frequently

People who are happy will genuinely be happy for you when you make it big or achieve your goal. Surrounding yourself with unsuccessful people and then talking about your successes will only remind these people of what they don't have. By contrast, surrounding yourself with people that have more than what you have you will make you feel more gratitude frequently. Gratitude is the attitude that brings success.

For example, if you achieved your goal in achieving a healthy, physically toned body, you're not going to be telling this to someone who is overweight (by choice) right? Because that person will only think you are bragging and wont share in your good fortune.

2. You get to be someone you've never been

In order to do something you have never done before, you need to stop caring about what people think of you. You need to realize that you cannot be doing the same things you have done if you want to become someone better. Surrounding yourself with people who want to achieve the same goal as you can make you do things you otherwise will not do. Successful people recognize that change is inevitable and that it must take place. Unsuccessful people will begrudge the changes in you whereas successful people will be glad that it happened and welcome it.

Chapter 5- Building and Mastering Emotions

Being aware of our emotions also means knowing that our emotions can drive our behavior and impact those around us, either positively or negatively. It also means we have the ability to manage these emotions, that of our own and that of others, especially at pressuring and stressful times.

The Five Categories of Emotional Intelligence (EQ)

When it comes to Emotional Intelligence, there are five categories that becomes a focus.

1. **Self-awareness.**

Having self-awareness means having the ability to recognize an emotion as and when it occurs and it is the key to your EQ. In order to develop self-awareness, a person needs to tune into their own true feelings, evaluating them and subsequently managing them.

In self-awareness, the important elements are:

- Recognizing our own own emotions and its effects
- Having a level of confidence and sureness of your capabilities and your self-worth

2. **Self-regulation.**

When we experience emotions, we often have little control over our actions when we first feel these emotions. One thing we can control however is how long these emotions last. To control how long certain emotions last, especially negative ones, certain methods are used to lessen the effects of these emotions such as anxiety, anger and even depression. These methods include reinventing a scenario in a much positive manner such as through taking a long walk, saying a prayer and even meditating.

Self-regulation includes:

- Innovation which means open to new ideas
- Adaptability to handle change and be flexible
- Trustworthiness referring to the ability to keep to standards of integrity and honesty
- Taking responsibility, conscientiousness of our own actions
- Self-control to prevent disruptive impulses

3. **Motivation**

Having motivation is what keeps us going to accomplish our tasks and goals and to maintain an air of positivity. With practice and with effort, we can all program our minds to be more positive although as human beings, it is also good to be negative at times. This does not mean having negative thoughts are bad, but these thoughts need to be kept in check as they cause more harm than good. Whenever you feel like you have negative feelings, you can also reprogram them to be more positive or at least to pick out the positive aspects of the situation, the silver lining which will help you be more focused in solving the problem.

Motivation is made up of:

- Having the sense of achievement drive, to constantly strive to improve and meet a level of excellence.

- Having the commitment to align your individual, group or organizational goals
- Having the initiative to act on available opportunities
- Having the optimism to pursue your goals persistently and objectively, despite the setbacks and obstacles.

4. Empathy

Empathy is the ability to recognize how people would feel towards a certain scenario, thing or person. Having this ability is crucial to success both in career as with life. The more you can decipher the feelings of people, the better you can manage the thoughts and approaches you send them. Empathetic people are excellent at:

- Recognizing, anticipating and meeting a person's needs
- Developing the needs of other people and bolstering their individual abilities
- Taking advantage of diversity by cultivating opportunities among different people
- Developing political awareness by understanding the current emotional state of people and fostering powerful relationships
- Focusing on identifying feelings and wants of other people

5. Social skills.

Developing good interpersonal skills is imperative as well if you want a successful life and a successful career. In our world today when plenty of thing are digitized, social skills seem to be an afterthought. People skills are more relevant and sought-after then before especially since now you also need a high EQ understand, negotiate and empathize with others especially if you deal and interact with different people on a daily basis. Among the most useful skills are:

- Influence to effectively wield persuasive tactics
- Communication to send our clear and concise messages
- Leadership to inspire and guide people and groups.
- Change catalyst in kick-starting and managing change
- Managing conflicting situations which includes the ability to negotiate, understand and resolve disagreements
- To bond and nurture meaningful and instrumental relationships
- Teamwork, cooperation and collaboration in meeting shared goals
- Creating a synergetic group to work towards collective goals.

Creating a Balance with Emotional Awareness

As a human being, emotions and feelings make up every aspect of our existence. Managing them and keeping them balanced will help us reach our maximum potential in life, at work and especially in our relationships. As we know by now, having good emotional balance leads us towards better physical and mental health, making life happier.

When our emotional well-being is disrupted, this will result in the opposite. Our physical health will decline, we will start having digestive problems, lack of energy and sleep issues. People with emotional distress often exhibit low self-esteem, they are self-critical and pessimistic. They always need to assert themselves through their behavior. They are overly worried, get afraid very fast and they are focused on the past.

- Connection between our Thoughts and Feelings

Thoughts determine our feelings and they are nothing more than firing the neurons in our body. Our thoughts also generate feelings, making our body release additive natural substances such as cortisol and adrenaline.

The connection between the body and the mind is extremely vivid and strong, strong enough that the mental and physical state sends positive and negative vibes both ways. The feelings we experience depends on our thought, combined with our attitudes and actions.

Emotions are part of our daily life and we experience this everyday. What we want is to strike a balance in our emotions, thoughts and feelings to ensure that they do not adversely affect our daily tasks and cause us stress.

- **Creating Emotional Balance**

So how we do create emotional balance? Emotional balance is the ability to maintain equilibrium and flexibility between the mind and body when we are faced with changes or challenges. Here are some ways that you can create emotional balance:

1. Accept your emotions

Many of our mental, emotional and physical problems stem from our inability to express ourselves emotionally. When we experience an emotional distraught, we smother it in the comforts of eating, sleeping, sweating it out, sucking it up, it is swept under a rug, we bury it, project it elsewhere, meditate even all in the hopes of suppressing our emotions instead of actually dealing with it by accepting that this is what we are going through right not. The key here is to allow ourselves unconditional permission to feel- to cry when we want to, to feel anger when we are angry, sadness when we grief and so on. Let your guard down either when you are alone or with someone you trust and just focus on the feeling and situation. Experience and immerse yourself in this feeling so you can comprehend better why it hurts and what you will be doing to remedy the situation once you've accepted and acknowledge these feelings.

2. Express yourself

Expressing yourself is important. There are many ways to express oneself and usually when we experience a feeling, we react by crying, shouting, throwing things. But to identify with ourselves and be able to manage our emotions properly, we can also express ourselves through more positive ways. Some people like reading as it provides an escape into a different world. Some people express themselves through art or music. Whatever it is that you do, make sure you stay connected to discover more about yourself, your identity and also the person you want to become.

3. Don't shove your feelings

Sometimes, it is easy to shove our feelings and not think about it, especially painful and scary memories. But as we all know, stuffing your memories and feelings will only make things worse for you. While it is hard to address your fears and sadness, rage and anger, once you actually dive into it, you will find that it will become easier to face your fears and eventually, the choppy waters will become calmer.

Be accepting your past and dealing with it in a more emotional state, you ultimately will lead a harmonious life. Always allow yourself to feel because your reactions to these different feelings would be in a more stable way rather than an overreaction.

4. See the world in a positive light

It is easier said than done, we know. In a world full of hatred, sadness, grief, war, crime, unfairness- it is a threat to our emotional health. You tend to develop low self-esteem and start asking yourself if you are worth it, if you can get through it, if you are doing things right and all these thinking steers you towards making more mistakes and missteps. Rather than having emotional self-doubt, take action to develop a prerogative of seeing the world in a more positive light.

Do not feel responsible for the bad things that happen which is not caused by you is a good start. Have compassion in yourself and practice mindfulness and accept that occasional lapses and failures are just part of being human.

5. Get a grip on your mind

The way we think causes us emotional distress- this probably is not news to you. We all have this tendency into overthinking and these thoughts that do not serve you or give you any positivity is just setting you up for emotional distress. So get a grip on your mind- do not let it wander to much especially when you start overthinking.

6. Practice Yoga and Mindfulness

Doing yoga on a daily basis does help in your mental health- it helps by increasing your confidence in your abilities and it also helps you make better, definitive decisions.

You also learn to not be so self-criticizing. Yoga, practiced on a daily basis can help get rid of negative energy within you and help you work your way towards mental clarity and vital energy.

Not only that, the breathing that is practiced in yoga helps you relax better, make you calmer especially if your mind is racing and it also helps you to refine your feelings.

Breathing correctly helps you get rid of stress and anxiety as well.

Conclusion

While emotional balance is vital, just remember that it is alright to have emotional imbalance so do not beat yourself up over it and overthink things. However, do not neglect this imbalance. If you feel you are emotionally imbalanced, do something about it either talk to someone you trust, meet a therapist or just find a positive way to express your emotions and feelings. Live a life without or little regrets.

Chapter 6- Practical Steps for Becoming Self Compassionate

Self-compassion is necessary for a healthy relationship, healthy mind and healthy body. How we interact with people and how we think affects how our body responds too. Self-compassion is the practice of goodwill and not good feelings. To practice self-compassion, we have first and foremost, change the way we think and perceive things. We also need a little bit of faith and believe in ourselves, in our strengths, in the way our life is heading, our goals and our priorities.

In this chapter, we will look at:

- the power of faith and believe in changing our perceptions
- practising creative visualization
- Practising affirmations
- **Faith & Believe**

When someone says 'Have faith' this depends on what you view or think what faith is. For many people, faith can be many different things and in all honesty, there's no right or wrong.

Conventionally, a lot of people associate faith with spirituality or the faith in God and that's not wrong either but like mentioned above, the very fact that people have different perspectives of what faith is is a good thing! It is quite enlightening and helpful to plenty of individuals that faith has different meanings as it can help different people make clearer sense of the various spectrums of life.

Here's a quick guideline to what faith means:

- **Faith**

Faith can mean faith in a supreme being, in God. But psychologists of religion would say that this is more of belief. Faith, in a more naturalistic and psychological sense, is really about the innate sense to search for meaning, purpose, and significance. Every human person has a strong sense that there is more than what meets the eye. In other words, there is something more than just 'me' and as human beings, we all discover what this might be- some of us go all out while some of us are content with the information we have at the moment.

All of us human beings seek out to find the deeper meaning, purpose and significance that exist in our lives, in our relationships and all the things that occur around us. This is the very basic striving of faith and the universal role it plays in our lives.

Wikipedia describes faith as a trust or confidence on a person, element or thing. Faith also is connected to the observation of an obligatory process that creates loyalty or even fidelity to a person, a promise or engagement. Faith is also a belief that is not based on facts and proof and faith can also mean loyalty to a system of religious belief.

While we think that only people that belief in divine intervention or God seem to have faith, the thing is even atheists have this kind of faith- a belief or trust or confidence. Everyone has the gift of faith- some of us have strong faith while some of us have weaker faith, but it really depends on the context we talk about.

- **Belief**

This brings us to the next element- belief. Belief is a representation of truth claims that you make on your spiritual journey. Beliefs are what tell you what is true and what is not true, and this is based on your experiences to satisfy your sense of faith. Your beliefs are what your hold to be true in your journey to satisfy your faith by engaging in various spiritual pursuits such as pilgrimage.

- **The Value of Faith**

While we all like to think we have faith (and high levels of it) the truth is, the value of our faith only grows when we are faced with troubling times. Many people believe that their faith value is determined by the evidence of things or successful moments or achievements in life. But the value of faith only increases as we grow older, as we experience more and more things in life, some good and some bad. Our faith becomes more valuable as we go through the trials and testaments of life and its heartaches. It is only during these times that you truly understand the depth and strength of a person's faith.

- **The Difference between Faith & Belief**

Probably by reading this now, you'd come to deduce that faith and belief are not the same things. In fact, in most cases, faith and belief are entirely the opposite of each other. Confusion between these two elements is tested when you face a crisis. While you may be searching for faith in something at a moment of crisis, you may be only pulling out the various beliefs that you have.

So the question is, who are you if not for your convictions?

If you have gone through a terrible crisis in life, you are probably still trying to figure it all out. Some people take years to understand why what happened to them, happened. Many people, especially those who are religious, feel the need to leave their faith in God because they believe that God has abandoned them.

But the questions are, were you abandoned by God or were you abandoned by your beliefs?

- **Belief as a product of the Mind**

A negative mind is already at a disadvantage but even a healthy mind can run into its own set of problems. For the enabled mind, a person may think that because they pray to God, all their prayers will be answered and that God is just and he will set things right. The positive mind will say that if we hold on to our beliefs strongly, God listens and will favor us.

But what is it that we believe in? Our beliefs are rooted in our culture and our upbringing. This is the first thing that separates our faith from our belief. Oftentimes, what we belief in may directly contradict everything else we know to be true and right. It can be universally acknowledged that we arrive at the crossroads of faith and belief when we go through a life-threatening crisis ourselves and when this happens, we end up changing our stronghold beliefs.

Changing our minds to adapt to crises is to change some part or elements of our beliefs. It is perfectly normal to shift our beliefs because our beliefs are modeled on personal and communal experience. A belief can necessarily be not true even when it has been handed down to us. In other words, a belief is not necessarily the only truth.

- **Belief is a product of the mind, faith is not**

Faith is the product of the spirit. Our mind also has a tendency to interfere with the process of faith rather than contributing it. To have confidence in the most depressing of times will require us to quiet the mind because the mind can run amok when we let it, especially when we have every negative thought clouding our mind.

Faith comes in when our beliefs run aground. Be wary that our beliefs can sway our spirit. Think of Galileo and how everyone thought the world was flat until he came around to prove that the world was indeed round. The belief that we humans have held for centuries can come and go over the course of a millennium.

- **Beliefs come and go**

But our faith is not as fickle as our belief. True faith is not a statement of our beliefs, but it is a state of being. Faith is trusting beyond all reasonable doubt and beyond all evidence that you have not been abandoned. Faith is achieved through commitment and to commit to faith is not the same thing as committing to a series of beliefs. When we are in the moment of crisis, faith tells us it doesn't matter whether its God or circumstances. To not know in the perspective of faith is to remain humble and open to learning. When faith does not fill in the cracks in a crisis, then fear will. Therefore, faith is an attitude that we create where it is the acceptance of not knowing. Unknowing is what creates faith.

Practicing Creative Visualization to Encourage Self-Compassion

Creative visualization is a mental technique that harnesses our imagination to make our goals and dreams a reality. When used the right way, creative visualization has been proven to improve the lives of the people who have used it, and it also increases the success and prosperity rate of the individual. Creative visualization unleashes a power that can alter your social and living environment and circumstances, it causes beneficial events to happen, attracts positivity in work, life, relationships, and goals.

Creative visualization is not a magic potion. It uses the cognitive processes of our mind to purposely generate an array of visual mental imagery to create beneficial physiological, psychological or social effects such as increasing wealth, healing wounds to the body or alleviating psychological issues such as anxiety and sadness. This method uses the power of the mind to attract good energy and really, it is the magic potion behind every success.

Mostly, a person needs to visualize an individual event or situation or object or desire to attract it into their lives. This is a process that is similar to daydreaming. It only uses the natural process of the power of our mind to initiate positive thoughts and natural mental laws. Successful people like Oprah and Tiger Woods and Bill Gates use this technique, either consciously or unconsciously, attracting success and positive outcomes into their lives by visualizing their goals as already attained or accomplished.

- **The Power of Thoughts and Creative Visualization**

So how does this work and why is it so important to us?

Well, our mind is a powerful thing. With only the power of our mind, we can reach amazing success, or we can also spiral out of control. It swings both ways. Our subconscious mind accepts the ideals and thoughts that we often repeat, and when our mind accepts it, then your mindset also changes accordingly, and this influences your habits and actions. Again, a domino effect happens where you end up meeting new people or getting into situations or circumstances that lead you to your goal. Our thoughts come with a creative power that can mold our life and attract whatever we think about.

Remember the saying that goes 'mind over matter?' When we set our mind to do it, our body does what our mind tells us. Our thoughts travel from mind, body, and soul but believe it or not; it can travel from one mind to another because it is unconsciously picked up by the people you meet with every day and usually, most of the people you end up meeting are the ones who can help you achieve your goals.

You probably think and repeat certain thoughts everyday pretty often, and you probably do this consciously or unconsciously. You probably have focused your thoughts on your current situation or environment and subsequently, create and recreate the same events and circumstances regularly. While most of our lives are somewhat routine, we can always change these thoughts by visualizing different circumstances and situations, and in a way, create a different reality for you to focus on new goals and desires.

- **Changing Your Reality**

Honestly, though, you can change your 'reality by changing your thoughts and mental images. You aren't creating magic here; all you are doing is harnessing the natural powers and laws that inhibit each and every one of us. The thing that separates normal, average folk with wildly successful people is that the successful ones have mastered their thoughts and mental images while the rest of us are still learning or trying to cope. Changing your thoughts and attitude changes and reshapes your world.

Take for example you plan on moving into a larger apartment and instead of wallowing in self-pity such as the lack of money, do this instead- alter your thoughts and attitude and visualize yourself living in a larger apartment. It isn't difficult to do because it's exactly like daydreaming.

- **Overcoming Limited Thinking**

You may think daydreaming about positive things and money and success and great relationships are nothing but child's play but in fact, creative visualization can do wonders. Though that, it may be hard for different individuals to immediate alter their thoughts. Limits to this positive thinking are within us and not the power of our mind- we control it.

It might sound like its easy to change the way you think, but the truth is, it takes a lot of effort on your side to alter your thoughts at least in the immediate future. But never for a second doubt that you can't. Anything that you put your mind to work on, it can be done.

We often limit ourselves due to our beliefs and our thoughts and to the life we know. So the need to be open-minded is an integral part of positive thinking. The bigger we dare to think, the higher and great our changes, possibilities and opportunities. Limitations are created within our minds, and it is up to use to rise above all these obstacles.

Of course, it takes time to change the way we think and see things and broaden our horizons, but small demonstrations of changing our minds and the way we think will yield bigger results in due time.

- **Guidelines for Creating Visualization**

Concise Guidelines for Creative Visualization:

Step 1: Define your goal.

Step 2: Think, meditate and listen to your instinct, ensure that this is the goal you want to attain

Step 3: Ascertain that you only want good results from your visualization, for you and for others around you.

Step 4: Be alone at a place that you will not be disturbed. Be alone with your thoughts.

Step 5: Relax your body and your mind

Step 6: Rhythmically breathe deeply several

Step 7: Visualize your goal by giving it a clear and detailed mental image

Step 8: Add desire and feelings into this mental image- how you would feel etc

Step 9: Use all your five senses of sight, hearing, touch, taste and smell

Step 10: Visualize this at least twice a day for at least 10 minutes each time

Step 11: Keep visualizing this day after day with patience, hope and faith

Step 12: Always keep staying positive in your feelings, thoughts and words

Staying positive can be easy, it is all about training your mind. When you do feel doubts, and negative thoughts arise, replace them with positive thoughts. Also remember to keep an open mind because opportunities come in various ways so when you see it, you can take advantage of them. Every morning, or each time you conclude your visualization session, always end it with this 'Let everything happen in a favorable way for everyone and everything involved.'

Creative visualization will open doors but it takes time and whenever you feel you are in a position of advantage, take action. Do not be passive or wait for things to fall on your lap. Perhaps you've met someone who can put yours in a position of advantage to reach your goal or perhaps you've landed a job that has the possibility of enabling you to travel. All these things come into your life, and if you have an open mind, you can see the possibilities more vividly.

When you use the power of imagination for you and the people around you, always do it for good. Never try creative visualization to obtain something forcibly that belongs to others (like someone else's husband or wife or a managerial position someone else rightfully achieved but you want as well). Also, don't harm the environment.

Most visualized goals happen in a natural and gradual manner, but there can be times that can happen in a sudden and expected manner too. Be realistic with your goals, though. Don't visualize a unicorn and expect it to turn up. If money is what you desire, you know that it just will not drop from the sky. You may or may not win it in the lottery. But the chances or possibilities are higher when you go through life with a new job, or you get a promotion, or you end up making a business deal.

It is always better to think and visualize what you actually want because you do not want to attract situations that are negative, in your quest to fulfill your goals and desires.

Using Affirmations

Affirmations have helped many people make significant changes in their lives and the people around them. Do they work for everyone? Why do some people have achieved success using this technique but some people do not get anything from it?

- **What are Affirmations?**

Affirmations are positive and direct statements that help an individual overcome self-sabotaging and negative thoughts. It helps a person visualize and believe in their goals, dreams, and abilities. In other words, you are affirming to yourself and helping yourself make positive changes to your life goals. Affirmations have the power to work because it can program a person's mind into believing a concept. The mind is known not to know the difference between what is real or fantasy. That is why when you watch a movie; you tend to empathize with the characters on the screen even though you know it's just a movie. But as soon as you leave the cinema, you are back into reality but can't help feel sorry or happy for the characters.

There are both positive and negative affirmations and some of these affirmations such as being told you are smart when you were a child or being told that you are clumsy can stick with us in both our conscious or unconscious mind. When we face failure, we tend to over-calculate the risks we are taking and work out the worst possible scenario which is usually the emotional equivalent of our parents or guardian deserting us.

We imagine an entirely dreadful scenario in our minds that we convince ourselves that trying to change isn't a good thing at all. Thus, it makes us lose out on opportunities for success and then when we actually do fail (because our mind is already convinced we'll fail anyway) the whole experience of affirmation that we give ourselves is that we are not cut out for success, or it is not in our karma to succeed, and then, we settle.

If a negative belief is firmly rooted in our subconscious mind, then it will have the ability to override any positive affirmation even when we aren't aware of it. This is one of the reasons why people do not believe in positive affirmations because it doesn't seem to be working. Their negative patterns are so high it just knocks out the sun!

So how do we add affirmations into our daily life and how can we make them prevail above our negative thinking? Here are some steps to follow:

Making Affirmations Work for You

Step 1- On a day that you are alone and not busy or distracted (if you don't have a time like this, then make one) list down all your negative qualities. Include any criticism that others have made of you and those that you have been holding onto. Remember that we all have flaws so do not judge. By acknowledging your mistakes, you can then move forward and work on your flaws, and you can make a shift in your life. When you write these down, take note to see if you are holding any grudges along the way or holding on to it. For example, do you feel tightness or dread in your heart?

Step 2- Begin to write out an affirmation on the positive aspect of your self-assessment. Use powerful statement words to beef up this assessment. Instead of saying 'I am worthy' say 'I am extremely cherished and remarkable.'

Step 3- Practice every day reading this affirmation loudly for five minutes at least three times a day in the morning, afternoon and at night before going to sleep. You can do this while shaving or putting your make up on, or when you are fixing yourself a cup of tea or if you are in the shower. At best, look in the mirror, so you look at yourself and repeat these positive statements. You can also write these affirmations in your notebook at any time you feel like it. Take note of how your writing changes over time. If we do not like something, often writing this down will encompass using smaller handwriting but if we right in big and bold letterings, we are increasing the affirmation of this. This is really a mindfulness journey to get to the agenda of positive affirmation.

Step 4- To enhance the impact, do body movements such as placing your hand on your heart when you felt uncomfortable writing out a negative criticism of yourself in Step 1. As you work on reprogramming your mind to alter it from the concept of affirmation to a real and definite personification of the quality that you see.

Step 5- Get someone to help you repeat your affirmations. This can be a friend or a gym coach or just about anyone that you feel safe with. For example, if they are saying that you are cherished and remarkable, and then connect this statement with your situations such as 'excellent colleague' or 'good fathering.' If you are not comfortable with doing this with someone, then look at your reflection in the mirror and reinforce your positive message.

Affirmations can be an incredibly powerful tool that can help you change your state of mind, alleviate your mood and more importantly, ingrain the changes your desire into your life. But for all of this to happen, you first need to identify the negative and the work on getting rid of them in your life.

Examples of Positive Affirmation

Here are some examples of positive affirmations that you can use to relate to the various areas of your development:

- I know, accept and am true to myself
- I believe in myself and have confidence in my decisions

- I eat a balanced diet, exercise regularly and get plenty of rest
- I always learn from my mistakes
- I know I am capable of anything and can accomplish anything I set my mind to
- I have flaws and I am not perfect but that's ok because I am human
- I never, ever give up
- I can adapt and accept what I have no control over
- I make the best of every situation
- I always look at the bright side of life
- I enjoy life to the fullest
- I stand up for what I believe in, my morals and my values
- I treat others with respect and recognize their individuality
- I can make a difference
- I can practice understanding, patience and compassions
- I am always up to learn new things and be open-minded
- I live in the moment and learn from my past and prepare for my future

These are just some of the positive affirmations that you can use to be optimistic and pursue a fulfilling and happy mindset. Have fun in creating your own affirmations or tailor the above to suit your needs and situation. Most of the affirmations above can be used daily to uplift, inspire and motivate you and those around you.

Mindfulness Meditation for Self-Compassion

Have you thought about meditation or have you done meditation before? Meditation does wonders to your body, mind and soul. When it comes to practising self-compassion, mindful meditation helps you incorporate this into your daily life more frequently. Keep in mind that mindful meditation isn't only helpful for self-compassion but it also helps us deal with the negativity that we face when we want to practice self-compassion.

Exercise 1 – Mindful Breathing

Breathing is an essential part of the meditative experience, so it is only natural that we should

exercise this too. Whenever you meditate, you're breathing mindfully when you focus on each purposeful breath that goes in and out of your body. Mindful breathing doesn't just have to happen when you're meditating, it can be done anywhere and at any time whether you're sitting, standing or just walking about. Make it a habit to breathe mindfully and you'll find it much easier to do so during your meditation sessions.

1. Start by bringing your attention and focus to your breathing.
2. Breathe in slowly for approximately 3 seconds, and then release that breathe slowly, counting to 3 seconds again.
3. During this exercise, you should focus and be thinking of nothing else except your breathing. Do not think about the tasks you need to do, or a meeting that is coming up at work. Think about

nothing but your breathing in and out, counting the seconds as you do.

4. Concentrate on the air that is filling your lungs as you breathe in, the way it makes your body feel, and when you release your breathe, imagine all the stress and the tension leaving your body as you do.

You can do this for 1-2 minutes at a time throughout the day, several times a day and you're already on your way towards improving each meditation session when you get better at learning to control your breathing.

Exercise 2 – Awareness

When you meditate, you learn to become more aware of your body, your mind and your thoughts, aware of what is happening all around you when your eyes are closed because your other senses become heightened when your eyes are shut. Being mindfully aware helps you sharpen your focus and remain alert to not just your surroundings, but your thoughts as well. For example, if you were mindfully aware about your thoughts, you will have better control when it comes to keeping any negative thought or emotion at bay.

Exercising your awareness throughout the day will help sharpen your alertness towards everything around you. Not just around you, but within you too. Beginners often find focusing on awareness to be a struggle in the beginning, because its so easy to let our thoughts drift and get distracted by everything else. Training yourself to be more aware will help you better connect your mind and body during your meditation sessions, so it's a good idea to practice these throughout the day to help you sharpen your focus and cultivate a heightened sense of awareness.

1. Start by choosing an activity or an object to focus on. Pick something that you would normally do without thinking twice about it, like opening the door or getting dressed in the morning for example.
2. Once you've got your object or activity, start to really, actively pay attention to what you're doing. If you're opening the door, concentrate on it. Reach for the doorknob and be aware of how it feels in your hand, and the motion of pulling the door towards you or away from you. Stop and appreciate how lucky you are to be healthy and fit enough to walk out your front door with a destination and a purpose in mind.
3. When you're getting dressed in the morning, focus and be aware of what you're doing instead of just going through the motions. Concentrate on how the fabric of your clothes feel in your hand, and even stop to appreciate how fortunate you are to be able to have a selection of clothes to choose from as you go through your closet looking for something to wear.
4. Before you eat, be aware of the food that is in front of you, how good it smells, the shapes, the colors. As you take each bite and begin to chew, be aware of how the food tastes and you take each bite with purpose.

Eventually, being mindfully aware is something that will come much easier, and the more you practice the easier you will find it is to concentrate on what you're doing or thinking without becoming easily distracted by other thoughts around you.

Exercise 3 – Mental Focus

Successful meditation involves being able to concentrate and not let your thoughts get easily distracted, which means you're going to need to work on improving your focus. Exercises to improve your focus are simple enough, here's what you can do:

1. Pick an object to focus on and place it in front of you.
2. When you're ready, set a timer and start to focus on the object and nothing else.
3. Concentrate on that object and keep staring at it for as long as you can.
4. When your mind begins to wander, stop and make a note of how long you managed to concentrate on that object before your mind started to drift.
5. Next round, do the same thing but try to go for a longer time this time around, aiming to beat your previous record.

Gradually, you should be able to focus on the object in front of you for longer periods of time before you find yourself getting distracted. The longer you can focus on the object, the better your focusing abilities will become.

PART 2

Dialectical Behavior Therapy is a reinforcement that every life is worth living. This style of therapy is designed with your life in mind. These practices are not here to interrupt your well-being, but to reestablish what it is that you find wholesome and fulfilling about your life. This is a path that is ultimately led by yourself. This is your life at its fullest. The choices you make and new territories that you discover will be your own adventure, as set by your own path at your own pace. You have control over your own life, how exciting! By the end of this book, you will come to meet you as you in your most honest and most content being.

Chapter 1: Is This for You?

Before we start this adventure, we have to ask, who is this intended for? The short answer is that it is for everyone who wants to make a positive change in their lives. The key word there is "want". This is ultimately a choice. You must establish your own journey as the techniques exemplified in this book are just practices. There is no set number of meditation sessions that will unlock mindfulness. The practice of these techniques only increases the chances of your own self-discovery. Your willingness to find that goal is the only way these practices will be effective.

This may seem confusing or even overwhelming, but it should be celebrated! You have made a choice to better your life. You possess the bravery to examine yourself in your own state. You are already stronger for it. There is value in yourself and your life and you have already made the decision to discover yourself at your most honest, happiest state and to continue to not only endure but thrive in a world made by your own choices. The biggest step is the first one, and that step is already behind you. It is time to breathe a sigh of relief, to feel accomplished. The worst part of your journey is behind you.

Now that you have made the first step, where do you go? Obviously, the answer is your own choice. The practices in this book are merely there to help you along the way. This may or may not be a path that you have previously gone down, so use these techniques to guide you in your own journey. Look at this book as a toolkit. There is nothing in these pages that will assume a role of authority over you. That is the beauty of free will! You are free to explore at your own pace in your own order.

"Often, it's not about becoming a new person, but becoming the person you were meant to be, and already are, but don't know how to be."

— Heath L. Buckmaster, Box of Hair: A Fairy Tale

You have already made the most important step, and that step is the one that separates you from your furthest setbacks. There is already so much distance between where you were and where you are now. It is now possible to look back and accept yourself. Standing where you are now, it is possible to see your own worth. You are not your setbacks, and you are not your failures. In fact, you might be the most interesting person you know!

Chapter 2: Your Toolbox, DBT

The goal of Dialectical Behavior Therapy (DBT) is to separate you from behaviors that are harmful to yourself and others and replace them with meaningful habits. Now that you have taken your first step and have separated yourself from your setbacks, you can go even further and discover what it is that makes you truly happy on your own. Finding that you do not live to continue harmful behaviors but discovering and tailoring habits that will enhance the life that you are choosing to live will fill you with serenity and self-love, and it will be all the more meaningful because they will be your own interests and not the consequences of your setbacks. Honestly, how exciting is it to really discover the real you? Someone that you may have never met or may not have seen in a long time and neither has anyone else, a brand-new person who has been there all along.

The defined objectives of DBT is obviously a little more clinical. It includes Mindfulness, Distress Tolerance, Interpersonal Effectiveness, and Emotion Regulation. How does this relate to you, though? How do these skills fit into your new and exciting life? Remember that the goal of this kind of therapy is not to overtake your life, but to be there alongside it to help you discover what it is that makes you the real you.

Mindfulness is not a skill set, more so a state of being. Mindfulness is being aware of the present, in the present, and not to be overwhelmed by what is going on around you. It is an awesome way to be and reinforces who you are because only you have a mind like yours. Whenever you are using your senses to become directly aware of your present state of being, you are being mindful. Mindfulness is also exercised like a muscle. It is something that we all possess, but few regularly practice. Although that statement may not be true for long. There is a growing interest in meditation and a growing awareness of the importance of remaining mindful in every aspect of life from personal to even business. If you were to practice it, you will discover that the feeling of mindfulness becomes stronger the more you exercise that mental muscle. Focus and personal honesty will become stronger as you develop along this path. It is an exciting tool of self-discovery and one that will be explored upon later in this book.

Distress Tolerance is a measurement. It is your ability to accept distress that cannot be changed. Emotional pain is measured on a different scale altogether from physical pain, but it can be just as, or even more, damaging. The real skill here is learning how to find your own way around the distress and accept what you are unable to change. Practicing mindfulness will help you to separate yourself from distress factors but coming to terms with the reality of these stressful situations will no longer be a roadblock, but a defining challenge that will make you stronger and give you skills for future distress management.

"Grant me the serenity, to accept the things I cannot change; courage to change the things I can; and wisdom to know the difference."

Learning the difference between what you can and cannot control is paramount. Once you have accepted the reality of a stressful situation that you cannot control, you cease to try to change it but begin to find a path to live around or through it. Sometimes, the energy spent trying to change an unchangeable situation is more stressful than the original event! You owe it to yourself to not harm yourself. There are even times when the situation only seems to be so stressful because you have spent all of your energy and effort trying to change it instead of taking a step back and accepting it for what it is. You could even come to realize that the situation is more benign than how you have built it up to be inside your head. Sometimes, you can even find a way to turn it into a positive situation! You will never be able to do any of that if you are too busy stressing about the original situation, though.

Interpersonal Effectiveness will help you to build and maintain important relationships, including the one you have with yourself, as well as help you to define priorities and to arrange them in a sensible manner to live your new life the most effective. The clinical method is through the acronym DEAR MAN:

- **D**escribe the current situations
- **E**xpress your feelings and opinions
- **A**ssert yourself by asking for what you want, or by saying no
- **R**eward the person – let them know what they will get out of it
- **M**indful of objectives without distractions (attack the problem, not the person)
- **A**ppear effective and competent
- **N**egotiate alternative solutions

These are effective and healthy steps for conflict resolution and a great tool to have in mind to keep your communication on track and working towards an agreeable solution.

Respect is a trait valued by everybody in one way or another. Respect is earned and kept and can encourage stronger relationships with the important people in your life. Speaking in a respectful tone will lead you to your interpersonal goals in a way than getting agitated towards that person, situation, or even yourself. Self-respect is the true basis of interpersonal respect. Have you ever heard that you must learn to love yourself before you can love another? This is because you define for yourself, and exemplify to others, what respect means to you. How you treat yourself will set the standard for how others will feel that they can treat you. A person who dresses nice and speaks warmly with peers will garner more respect than a person who shows little care for how they want to be treated. Self-respect is important, and you deserve it! You are already stronger for having taken this journey and your story is one that no one else has. You are worthwhile, interesting, and unique. Taking good care of yourself will tell others that you are a person who warrants respect. Another acronym that is helpful about self-respect is FAST.

- **F**air to myself and others
- No **A**pologies for being alive
- **S**tick to values (do not do anything you will regret later)
- **T**ruthful without excuses or exaggeration

You have heard the Golden Rule; treat others as you would like to be treated yourself. Well, that rule works the other way as well! Treat yourself as you would treat others. You deserve the same respect that you would show to others, so do not count yourself out or make sacrifices that make you feel uncomfortable. Be fair to yourself!

If you find that you apologize unnecessarily, stop it! Sometimes, people will tell you that you apologize too much, which only make you feel uncomfortable. You do not have to apologize for anything that you are not truly sorry for. You occupy the same space as your peers and you deserve the same level of respect.

What are your values? Do you know? In your current stage of rebuilding and discovery, your values may change, or you may discover that you have been violating your own values for a long time. With a renewed respect for yourself and a bright new path ahead of you, you are most likely to find out what is truly important to you. Find your core values and remember that you deserve respect. You do not have to apologize for your values and you do not have to compromise your values. Make your identity known and remember that you are valid.

Once you know who you are, what you value, and the fact that you deserve and possess self-respect, honesty becomes easy. You do not have to fabricate yourself to fit in or hide any unsavory traits that you may think that you possess. Your peers will respect an honest you. Honesty to yourself and others is the pinnacle of freedom. You are who you are and who you are is a strong, healthy, and an interesting person! Half-truths and flat out lies do little more than create stress for everyone involved, including yourself. A person with self-respect does not need to create an identity that they do not own. Breathe and relax because you are you!

Chapter 3: Finding Yourself through Mindfulness

Discovering yourself is exciting! It's a journey that is enviable. We have already defined mindfulness, so the next step is to discover how it is practiced and define what your individual goals are. It is important to remember to constantly ask yourself what you want to find in this book. Your individual goals are the goals of this text. What practitioners of mindfulness usually find is greater fulfillment, a deeper understanding of their selves, positive behavioral changes, and more importantly, less suffering.

As you continue down this path, it is important to remember what your truest intentions are because doubts will surface. Mindfulness will need to be practiced and exercised like a muscle. Minds are messy, prone to wandering, prone to doubt, and everyone examines themselves much harsher than their peers would. In the last chapter, you discovered what your values are and who you are as a person. You discovered that self-respect is worth having. Now, it is time to reinforce what you know about yourself and what you want to explore.

Before we get to the actual practices, it is important to note that the path to mindfulness is not linear. It is a little different for everyone and the only outside guide is a collection of experiences from others. The true guide is yourself. Do not fret. Do not succumb to doubt because you may or may not discover a path differently or find a truth not listed in this book. No one can know you as well as you can. Instead of reveling in the doubt or confusion, be excited! You are the first to discover your exact path and you are the first to find your own unique solutions to your setbacks.

At the same time, you may discover that these goals are even connected! As you discover greater fulfillment, you may connect it to lesser suffering, and from there, you may find that you exhibit better behavior and more success in your relationships. Understand that practicing separateness from your suffering could lead to accepting validation from your own positive thoughts and energy.

The most obvious exercise for practicing mindfulness is meditation. It is important to note that meditation is not passive. It is not simply sitting and relaxing with your eyes closed. It is an active exploration of your mind while providing yourself with the least resistance to your own self-discovery. You may not just drop right into it during your first session. An unpracticed mind has never explored in that way. You may not know how to look inward as your senses and instincts are conditioned to look outward for stimulation.

First, you must separate yourself from your reactions. You must understand what your automatic reactions to a stimulus such as stress and joy are and be aware of yourself at the moment that you act automatically. You are not your feelings. You are not your reactions. Imagine you are on the side of a road watching traffic pass back and forth. Every car is a stimulus, feeling, or reaction. You are separate from them and you must merely make a mental note of it, and then let it pass. Be aware of their existence and acknowledge them, but do not react to them. Eventually, your mind will become more still.

Another example is to imagine your mind like a still pool of water. Every thought and stimulus is a pebble dropped in that pool. Those pebbles create concentric ripples that expand outward, and then even out. If you reach into the water to grab that pebble, you will only create a splash and larger ripples. Eventually, the pebbles will slow, and your quietest realizations and truths will surface. Do not fear! This is your truest self. This is exciting and another great achievement along with your journey to a more peaceful and successful you. After those truths have passed without judgment, your pool of water will fall even more still. You will experience true serenity and discover the most honest definition of a quiet mind. This is peace.

To practice meditation, you must first dedicate time and space to your session. You do not need a special pillow or certain music or any equipment whatsoever, just time and space to practice. Sit in a comfortable position that you will not stress to maintain and close your eyes. Next, just acknowledge the moment as it is. Observe it without judgment or interaction. Just simply be in the moment without exerting effort or energy towards it. Pay attention to the sensations of air passing through your nostrils or the presence of sound in your ears. Let the moment pass through you as you sit peacefully in it. The goal is not simply to be calm, it is to be aware of the moment as it is happening right now without interaction or judgment. The next step is not so much a step, but a reassurance. Judgments will rise. It is inevitable, especially when you are first practicing. Remain calm and remain practicing. Do not succumb to doubt or frustration. Simply make a note of it, and let it pass. This is an excellent practice for learning how to move on from frustration or feelings of grudge in your waking life. If your mind wanders too far off of your initial concentration, keep returning to the sensation of your breath. Focus on the gentle sensation of the in and out of your breathing. Simply be in your awareness.

Meditation is a proven method to reduce stress, increase clarity, and can even positively rearrange your brain chemistry! You will notice your brain will have less chatter in your normal life, and you will be less prone to anxiety. It is a great practice for finding a "third way" around a conflict. It can even open up your creativity and lower your heart rate and blood pressure. As I have mentioned before, it has even begun to appear in modern business practices. Some higher up CEOs have adopted this daily practice to increase their creativity and productivity and reduce their stress level in the fast-paced environment that is business. Everyone from athletes to political figures to your average working man benefits from this simple practice.

If you chose to partake in this particular practice, you are unlikely to regret it. The next chapter will focus on advanced meditation techniques for when you discover that you like this new calmer, more focused you!

Chapter 4: Taking Mindfulness to the Next Level with Advanced Meditation Techniques

If you have chosen to give meditation a try, then congratulations! You should feel proud of yourself for having the courage to try something new. You should feel reinforced in your feelings of solidity in your new and healthy life. You have made an actual effort and have taken real-life actions! This is another moment to look at just how far you have come. How has meditation affected your life already? Do you feel a renewed clarity? This chapter will show you advanced techniques that you can practice to further expand your meditation practices.

An easy form of meditation that you can incorporate in your daily life is called a Walking Meditation. Obviously, this can be done simply while walking, or any form of ambulation that you use to get around. It is an action that you do naturally and has been for years. You probably learned how to walk before you learned how to read! This kind of easy, almost automatic and steady movement is a perfect environment to study your meditation practices.

First, you must stand up straight. Keep your back straight as you practice this. It is important to find the posture that is comfortable and promotes easy steps and focus. Next, place your hands together just above your belly button with your thumbs curled in towards your palms. This position promotes a comfortable posture that brings your focus to your center. Your arms are not swaying, and you feel self-contained and comfortable. Now, let your gaze drop slightly. This will also allow you to focus while being aware of where you are walking to. Just like with normal sitting meditation, try not to get lost in outside stimuli, just simply make a note of them and continue on with your focus inwards. Now, you are ready to take your first step. In the last section, I mentioned that breathing could be used to bring your focus back to your center. In this exercise, you will use your steady footfalls to create a rhythmic cadence for you to keep your central focus on. Notice, without interacting, the sensation of the ground on your feet (or whatever mode of transportation that you would use to get around on your own). Notice as the ground rolls from the back to the front of your foot. Notice the gentle bounce of your body as you move along. Now, do the same with the next step and the next. Make sure to walk at a slightly slower pace than usual. It is not necessary to move ridiculously slow, just make sure that it is at a pace where you are able to focus on your gentle and rhythmic movements and still move along at a comfortable speed.

Benefits of this style of meditation are that it allows you to further exercise your focus outside of the room or environment that you have become comfortable meditating in. It allows you to start connecting that focus to your daily life as you practice maintaining that focus during the natural and unpredictable distractions that occur just in a day out. You will also begin to appreciate the seemingly mundane aspects of your day, bringing focus and renewed eyes to aspects of this wonderful life that may have gone unnoticed or underappreciated previously. A cloud moving in front of the sun might bring certain effects to your attention like the changing colors or temperature of this temporary state. You might find a renewed appreciation for the sun and life in general. A gentle breeze might remind you of how temporary forces in your life are. A passing conversation might show you how calm, focused, and centered you are feeling in the moment versus how frantic and anxious the average person is in their daily life. You will discover all of these things while keeping your focus centered. It is important to not react to any of their thoughts, just simply recognize the existence of these thoughts, and let them pass naturally on their own. Bringing your meditation practices from your sterile environment to the waking world is an excellent practice for learning how to maintain and call upon this state of focus when there are events in your life that may be exciting or stressful.

The next technique is quite the opposite. Instead of walking, this technique is most effective while laying down, but it can be done in a sitting position. It is called a Body Scan, and it is used to focus on your physical wellbeing. It gives the sensation of infusing your body with a healing breath.

First, you must sit or lie in a comfortable position. Do not pick a position or surface that will become uncomfortable or distracting during your meditation. Once you are in a good position, place your hands on your stomach in the same manner in which you did during the Walking Meditation, just above your belly button in a comfortable position that brings your focus to the center of your body in a full rest. Once you are in this position, you might find it easier to focus if you close your eyes. Now, take a few deep breaths. Take note of the moment as you are in it, just like you have practiced in the basic meditation technique. Then bring your attention to your body. Notice the sensation and pressure of the floor or chair on your back or legs. Keep taking deep breaths, but this time, notice the invigorating life that fills your body when you inhale deeply and then feel a deeper sense of relaxation on every exhale. Fall deeper and deeper into your focused state with each incremental breath. You may start to notice more minute sensations such as your pulse under your skin, or little hairs standing up on your arm as your body becomes more relaxed and focus.

Now, bring your focus to your stomach area. If your stomach is tense, let it loose. You might even notice that your entire body relaxes as you release the tension in your stomach. Shift your focus from your stomach to your hands just above that area. See if you can allow your hands to soften even more. Feel your body relax even another level. Now, bring your focus to your arms. Let the tension loose in your shoulders. Let the tension loose in your biceps and forearms. After that, it is time to bring your focus to your neck. Let the muscles in your neck relax. It is perfectly acceptable to let your body shift as your muscles become systematically more relaxed. It is almost bound to happen as you are achieving new levels of relaxation. How relaxed you are now will make your initial assessment when you first lied down seem so distant.

After you have relaxed your neck, then it is time to focus on your jaw. Let that tension go. In your waking life, the average person carries extra tension especially in their jaw, shoulders, and fists without even realizing it. You might perceive yourself as relaxed when in actuality; you are much tenser than what is comfortable. This is one of those realizations that you come across through meditation that is an invaluable lesson that you have taught yourself. After you have rolled your relaxing focus over your entire body, take a mental snapshot of your body as a whole. Notice your body in the same way that you notice passing thoughts in the basic meditation technique. You may realize that your body is yours, but it is not you. Your body is a vessel and a tool for who you really are. That separation is important when you practice meditation. It is what allows you to examine thoughts without attachment. Take one more deep breath and allow your eyes to open, feeling a new sense of invigoration and relaxation.

Congratulations! With these three meditation techniques; the basic meditation, the Body Scan, and the Walking Meditation, you are able to perceive and react to thoughts and stimuli within your mind, your body, and your world in a healthy way. There is nothing that you should not be able to process using these techniques. You now have the tools to tackle any hardships along your journey. On top of that, you now have a new perspective that is exciting to explore as you find new hobbies, relationships, and life choices. Now even simple tasks like breathing, walking, or even just existing can be healing and full of positive energy!

The next chapter will focus on processing negative thought patterns in a healthy way. Now that you have this new perspective and new tools, it should be easy to separate yourself from negative thoughts that may surface from your past or present life. Do not fear! You are ready. You are stronger than you have ever been, and you can tackle any setbacks you have experienced, or are currently experiencing. Take a moment to celebrate where you are versus where you have been!

Chapter 5: Using Your New Tools to Process Negative Emotions

Negative emotions will occur. It is the inevitability that comes with the endless possibilities of life. You cannot reasonably expect to live your entire life and never feel sad, hurt, angry, betrayed, embarrassed, or any other emotion that can be perceived as negative. In this chapter, we will review the skills that you have learned to more effectively process your emotions when an inevitably negative emotion occurs. Through Dialectical Behavior Therapy, Emotion Regulation breaks down into three goals.

1. Understand one's emotions
2. Reduce emotional vulnerability
3. Decrease emotional suffering

The first step begins with a simple truth, and that is emotions are not bad. Even negative emotions are not something to just be avoided. It is impossible, and unhealthy to attempt, to avoid every negative emotion that you will come across in your life. Attachment to negative feelings is what causes real suffering. You learned from the last two chapters how to separate yourself from thoughts and emotions. You simply must acknowledge the emotion and/or event, and then let it pass. It is important to acknowledge these emotions, though. Try to define your emotions clearly. Using phrases like "I feel bad" does not give a clear understanding of how you are feeling. Instead of "bad", expand on that. Pinpoint it by saying you feel frustrated, depressed, anxious, or angry.

Understanding what and how you are feeling is integral to processing those feelings. It is also important to understand the difference between primary and secondary emotions.

Primary emotions are reactions to an outside stimulus, and secondary emotions are reactions to those primary emotions. For example, if you felt depressed later about being too angry at a friend, then anger would be the primary emotion while depression would be the secondary emotion. The secondary emotion is a judgment of the primary emotion. Learning how to acknowledge emotions without judgment is essential because secondary emotions are destructive. Also, learning how to process negative events without succumbing to negative emotions is very important. Maybe being angry at the friend was not the proper response when you could have used the DEAR MAN acronym in the second chapter of this book to properly resolve that event and those feelings in a way that would solve the issue and be beneficial to both you and your friend. Remember that emotions are not your identity. Emotions are there just to alert you to stimuli that are beneficial or problematic. How you process and express these emotions is entirely up to you.

Reducing emotional vulnerability will increase the stability of your emotions, simply put. In DBT, the methods for reducing emotional vulnerability is through action. It will teach you to create positive habits and experiences to balance out the negative feelings you might be feeling. An easy acronym to remember for this is PLEASE MASTER.

PL – represents taking care of your physical body and reducing or treating illness

E – eat a balanced diet

A – is for avoiding alcohol and drugs, which can only heighten or fabricate negative feelings

S – Sleep. It is important to get regular sleep

E – The last E is for exercise. Much like meditation, it will increase in benefits the more you practice.

MASTER – This one is the fun one. Master positive activities to increase your sense of well-being and accomplishment.

Your health affects your emotional state. This ties into the self-respect section that we talked about in the second chapter. You will feel much better physically and emotionally if you raise your standards of how you treat yourself. Getting regular sleep, exercise, and only treating your body and yourself to healthy food and activities will do absolute wonders for your confidence. This also includes avoiding alcohol and drugs. It is too easy to mask feelings with these substances, and as we have learned, that is not a healthy way to process those emotions. Avoiding emotions, especially with mind-altering substances, does not make those emotions go away. It is not a permanent solution, it only encourages you to chase that perceived temporary safety from those emotions while your body is developing an addiction to the actual substance. It is a trap and can only work to undo all of the work that you have already accomplished. Treat yourself better than that because not only do you have self-respect, but you deserve it.

Now, I am going to circle back to the PL portion of the PLEASE MASTER acronym. After you understand the steps necessary for taking care of your body, you will understand that it is important to monitor your body as a whole. This includes taking care of illnesses when they arrive. Illness is another inevitability of life. Much like emotions, it is important to process them in a healthy manner to avoid further damage. You deserve to live in a healthy body and you owe it to yourself to take care of yourself. Living in a healthy body will give you peace of mind. Knowing that at the end of the day, you are physically feeling healthy will put other situations in perspective and it will be one more positive that you can weigh against negative emotions when they occur. Along with exercise and meditation, you can choose to MASTER other positive activities in your life. Developing or rediscovering a hobby is exciting and can give new meaning and a new sense of accomplishment in your life!

After you have learned these skills, you are ready to learn how to decrease emotional suffering. In DBT, it is comprised of only two skills: Letting go and taking opposite action.

Letting go refers to what we have already learned, by using our mindfulness to process emotions in a healthy way by letting them pass without developing secondary emotions to attach to the primary emotions. Taking opposite action means engaging in actions that are in direct contrast to the negative feelings that you are experiencing. For example, instead of crying when a feeling of depression is acknowledged, try to stand straight, speak confidently, and react to the stimulus or event in a healthy way. This is not to ignore that emotion. It is an exercise to lessen the length and severity of the emotion. It is important to acknowledge emotions, but that does not mean that you have to be subordinate to them. You do not need to let emotions control how you think and act. It can also give you a new perspective on a situation that you may have reacted automatically too.

With these skills, coupled with the skills you have learned in the previous few chapters, you can process emotions internally in your mind, body, and everyday life and also express those emotions after you have processed them. Even more to add to that, you have developed a renewed sense of self-respect through self-care and new or rediscovered hobbies. You are now taking steps to replace negative habits and feelings with positive feelings and activities you enjoy and that are uniquely representative of you! You may start to feel that you are meeting the real you, a more positive and honest version of yourself, doing things that you enjoy.

Chapter 6: Defining Your Goals, Your Values, and Yourself

Now, instead of learning something new, it is time to reassess yourself after what you have already learned. Do you remember those goals and values that you defined for yourself at the beginning of this book? Well much like how we discovered new levels of relaxation during the Body Scan meditation, it is time to discover new levels of yourself. Maybe after you have practiced meditation and studied the different goals of DBT, your renewed sense of self and awareness can further sharpen your goals and expectations from your new life. It is even possible that you have already achieved and mastered some of your goals. If you have, then congratulations! It is time to reassess what is important to you and what you can get out of this book. If you have not achieved any of your goals yet, then do not worry! Hopefully, you have set expectations at a reasonable level and you are mindful of what you are able to achieve within yourself. It is good to have both long-term and short-term goals. It is important, even, to balance both so you are able to celebrate achievements along the path to a life-affirming goal that you may not have been able to achieve without taking that all important first step along this journey.

Each new skill you learn is a skill you would not have had if you would have maintained your negative feelings and habits. There are questions for you now that only you can answer. How is it that you feel? How do you feel in a general sense of wellbeing? How far along do you think you have traveled? You are most likely aware of your progress and it is good to celebrate along the way. These steps you are taking are not steps that any one person could take for you, no matter how influential or qualified. Just like how meditation and mindfulness is a study of you, the steps you have taken are entirely unique to you.

Having said all of that, it is important to allow positive feelings to be acknowledged and witnessed. Many have a hard time accepting themselves in their own achievements. Judgments upon oneself can absolutely be the harshest. It is easy for faults and negative feelings to seem large and overwhelming when you are standing so near to them. These negative feelings cause you to stress and can be impossible to simply ignore. This is why we learn to process those feelings and resolve them instead of trying in vain to ignore them. An unresolved negative feeling can trigger a survival response, which is why it is impossible to ignore said feelings. In this way, unresolved negative feelings make it near impossible to accept positive feelings about yourself.

Your body does not feel the need to react to positive feelings because it feels that the situation is resolved because it ended on a satisfying conclusion. Your body will tell you that your time and effort need to be spent resolving those negative feelings because they are triggering a survival response in you. Now that you have learned how to bring negative feelings to a positive and productive conclusion, it is now possible to accept your positive traits and individuality. It is even possible to meet yourself without those impossible stresses in your life. How exciting and life-affirming is that! How much better off are you now in relation to how you were before you took this journey?

Now, that you know your goals, and you know yourself, what are your values in your new life now? What have you learned that you could possibly maintain, or even teach others? Maybe you recognize the work that you have put in and are starting to recognize the results of hard work. Maybe you value patience and understanding because practicing meditation has taught you how to discover feelings that were always there, just buried. All this book can do is speculate and give examples to what you may be feeling. It is your unique journey that is your real teacher. You have taught yourself how to heal. You have taught yourself how to take the first step, and you have taught yourself how to recognize greatness within yourself.

Are there people in your life who would be proud of you for where you are now? If so, you should greet them and share your renewed sense of pride and clarity with them. It is reaffirming of your own sense of accomplishments to have it validated by those you love, those you admire, and those you respect. Sometimes, it can give a new perspective to emphasize with someone else and share a joyful feeling with them. You are no longer in a cave of your own misjudgments, both internal and external. You have established yourself out in the light. You can walk among the world with your head high instead of living in the past and inside of your own head. You see the world for how it actually is and not through the lens of prior transgressions or feelings of worthlessness. It is even possible to look back at how you used to exist and treat yourself and separate yourself enough from it that you can even brush it off. That is not you anymore. You are the real you now. You are the you that you were meant to be, a much happier and more honest you who recognizes real emotions instead of perceived injustices to yourself.

Chapter 7: Living in the Positive!

Now that you have created a positive atmosphere for your mind to exist in, you are probably feeling a new motivation and longing to explore the world in your new self. What do you do with all of this motivation? It is important to put this good energy to use as to not fall back into negative habits that your old self has come to reinforce. You are at a crucial step where you should give great importance to channeling this positive energy into positive habits.

Something that you can do for yourself is to continue to practice meditation and exercise. Your new positive life starts at your core. Your core being yourself. You have learned a renewed sense of self-respect and discovered some deep insight into yourself. Now, it is time to maintain it. You can continue to live positive as long as you take care of yourself. Imagine yourself in a fancy car. It can look nice on the outside, but if the engine is not kept in good condition, it will not function as intended. Every new positive action starts with a sense of wellbeing.

Other ways to maintain your emotional stability through practice is to find a creative outlet for your feelings. If you feel that you are the creative type of person, then you may already have some of these hobbies. You may even have hobbies that you have not visited in a long time. Picking up an old hobby can help you connect with who you were before you found yourself down a darker path. It can give you a sense that you are picking up where you left off and reassure you that this you is the real you. If you are not a creative person or have not found an interest in a hobby, then do not worry! Another way that you can strengthen your mental focus and reinforce this new positive you are to learn. Reading is a proven method to increase cognitive faculties and helps you to directly discover interesting perspectives that you may not have come to on your own independently. Maybe, you will even discover ways to learn about aspects of your life that you have put on hold. Projects and promises made to others and you can now be fulfilled because you are now breathing easy and have a new motivation for life.

Great! Now that you have a healthy and positive sense of wellbeing, you can further reinforce your new positive life by engaging in productive social activities. Before I get into examples of this, I want to further explore the benefits.

Giving back to your community outwardly shows that you want to be engaged with society. You recognize yourself as a part of a whole and you are devoid of an ego that alienates you from your peers. It is not a struggle for your individuality though; you have already explored and defined yourself to yourself. Now, it is time to show who you are to the world! A person who lives inside of their own negative thought patterns does not want to be a part of society. They will build their own mental walls to keep themselves from embarrassment, anger, shame, or any other negative thought patterns associated with social interaction. Maybe they feel that society owes them something. An overinflated ego is another trepidation to avoid. Now that you are free of all of these negative thought patterns, you can enjoy social interaction with a head held high and nothing to apologize for. Another key benefit that you may not have seen or realized before, is that doing something nice for others simply feels good. You are able to emphasize the happiness of others. Seeing a smile on another person's face that you have caused can feel so rewarding in ways that you have never felt before! Even for more selfish reasons, it feels good, as in the sense of being the hero of someone's day. It is a wholesome feeling. It is a feeling that is entirely guilt-free.

Some examples of positive social outings would be simple activities like volunteer work or attending or even participating in sports events. Maybe your place of employment has a softball league, or your colleagues enjoy disc golf. These are activities that directly give back to your community or peer group. These are higher levels of commitment, so if you are not ready for that quite yet, maybe you could try something a little less structured. Meeting trusted friends in a relaxed social environment could be a little bit more comfortable for you. Invite a friend, or a few friends, out for lunch or to a store of your common interests. This kind of setting makes for a good conversation that is not so personal if you are not ready for that. It is perfectly acceptable to take your time developing your social identity, as this step is very important. Meeting friends in this kind of setting can also help you learn more about your friends and even yourself! Maybe they have an interest that you did not even know that you had! Maybe you have a friend who is very interested in tabletop gaming, which might be an area of interest that you have never explored! Your friends and new interests will most likely lead you to new friends and even more positive and interesting activities. It is easy to get sucked into the positive life; all you have to do is take the first step!

Working within your comfortable level of commitment is essential, but it is also important to actually engage in these or similar activities. The goal of this section is to establish new positive habits to replace self-destructive habits. Just like how picking up and reading this book was a crucial first step, this is another crucial step. Do not fret though! This step is easier than what you would think. Most of the time, the fear associated with the activity is much worse than the actual activity, and you should know how to properly process negative thought patterns. All you have to do is breathe and take that step. Your friends, family, and colleagues will be more than happy to have you included.

It is important to establish positive relationships that engage in positive activities. It is also important to allow yourself to learn what positive social activities are. A common misconception, reinforced by advertisements and common television shows, is that all social activity takes place with alcohol. That is simply not true. In fact, the most productive and happiest people may rarely step foot in one of these establishments. As a side note, you may also be surprised at the money you save when you do not frequently visit these establishments, which brings me back to advertisements. That is why those media outlets pursue that lifestyle; it is purely to promote a lifestyle that will earn their company more money. In that respect, establish your own idea of happiness! Find out what it is that truly makes you happy! You are most likely to find that engaging with friends develops real bonds and promotes honest happiness. You are most likely to find that volunteer work, or even saying yes when someone asks for a favor, is more fulfilling than anything that you have experienced in your previous life.

You should feel proud of yourself for taking this step! Now that you are taking steps to not only better yourself, but to solidify and reinforce it with positive social activities, there is nothing that can get in your way on your path to being happier, more wholesome you! Once again, congratulations!

Chapter 8: How DBT Has Enhanced Your Life

Although this book has seemed to have an almost conversational flow, it has actually followed very closely to the five functions of DBT. As this book has mentioned before, the goal of this is not to assume an authoritative role over you, the reader. This book was designed to reinforce your own choices and merely give examples of positive living for those who may be unaware or fearful of how to live as such. Having said that, it is now time to relate what we have learned to the five functions of Dialectical Behavior Therapy. Before we do that, let's define what those five functions are.

- Enhance client's capabilities
- Improve the client's motivation
- Assure generalization to the client's natural environment
- Structure the environment
- Enhance the therapist's capabilities and support their motivation

The clinical way to go about enhancing your capabilities is to reinforce the skills of DBT. We have used many skills directly from the actual standard of DBT, such as the acronyms DEAR MAN, FAST, and PLEASE MASTER. These are acronyms that you would become familiar with if you were to attend a regular DBT session. We have also discussed important skills like practicing mindfulness and emotional regulation. These are also skills that you are most likely to encounter in an actual DBT session. This book has taken those lessons and broken them down for you to study, practice, and make into your own at your own pace by your own choices. Using these skills in your own life will only work to enhance the quality of your life and introduce you to lifestyles that mirror your interests, even those that you may not be aware that you have. This is an exciting time to be alive, and an exciting time for you!

The next function of DBT is the enhancement of the client's motivation. This book was designed to keep you motivated throughout, but it is not what was written or the speed in which you read it. The real motivation comes from you. You have rewarded yourself for picking up this book and sticking to it all the way to the end. By now, you deserve to have developed a sense of pride in making these positive changes in your life! There is no outside force that can motivate you to the extent that you can motivate yourself.

This book was written to be a companion to your own life. You are free to read or not read, follow or not follow, at your own pace. The fact that you have made it this far is something to be celebrated. It shows that you are honest in your desire to rid yourself of negative thought processes and self-destructive habits. There is not a single person or entity that is able to instill that level of motivation inside of you. You have shown that you are committed; not to this book or these processes, but you are committed to yourself. You have already taken better care of yourself than previously you might have thought possible. It is not only acceptable but appropriate to celebrate yourself at this time. This is a real achievement that you have accomplished, and one that many people take multiple tries to achieve. Some may not ever get to the level of clarity and health that you have already achieved for yourself. Once again, Congratulations!

The third function of DBT may seem confusing at first. It is to assure generalization to the client's natural environment. What that means is that this treatment, and this book, is designed to be a companion piece to live alongside without overtaking your life. This is not a program designed to put your life on hold. The effectiveness of this is that it promotes ease of transition into your new lifestyle while giving examples that are digestible by you because they relate to you, just as you are. It is easy to take this book with you and read it at your own pace or use the skills you have learned through a DBT session or in this book while you go about living your day-to-day life. There is no commitment besides the commitment that you have made to yourself and are comfortable with.

In an actual DBT session, they would address this function within the moment coaching. You would have access to a 24/7 phone number that you would be encouraged to call if you are having a hard time with applying the lessons to your life you would have learned during a session. This is an excellent tool, and if you were to attend a DBT session, I would strongly encourage you to feel free to use it. These coaches are not there to judge your choices. They understand the material and are also encouraged to process emotions without judgment. This is purely for the benefit of you! It is also encouraging to have outside motivation when your motivation might be hitting a low point. There is nothing to worry about though, just like the inevitability of sickness or negative thoughts, you cannot fault yourself for when your motivation is feeling weaker at the moment. Just relax, call that number, and celebrate yourself for making the positive choice at that moment when you may not have previously.

We are almost through the list here, I hope that you feel encouraged to continue. The fourth function of DBT is to structure the client's environment. This one can seem almost scary because you have gone this far along your own choices. There is nothing to fear though because this step is not designed to take away your choices, merely to help you and provide tools for you to make positive choices when you may not have previously. How a DBT session would go about doing that would be to assign you a case manager. This is someone who is dedicated to your case and is working with you to ensure your success.

An important aspect of this function is the thought process when accepting it. It is not there to control your lifestyle. When a client has made poor life choices and made a habit out of them, then they might not be aware of or be comfortable with lifestyle choices that are more positive and sustainable. You have already decided to live a positive life, now it is time to learn how. That is the purpose of this function. In DBT, there is a strong focus on replacing negative habits with more positive habits. This is because pure motivation has to be outwardly expressed and used for it to continue. Imagine your positive motivation as a match. You can light the match, and it will burn for a while. It is hot, it is bright. It has the potential to continue on, but it can only continue on if fuel is introduced to the match. Imagine this function of DBT as a pile of wood arranged for you in a fire pit, ready to be lit by your motivational match. Once you apply the match to the wood in the fire pit, then the fire burns much longer in a safe environment. Your motivation must be applied to a positive atmosphere to continue on. Your case manager or other individuals in your DBT session use this function to safely provide you with those structured, positive environments. Go forth and do well for yourself and others!

Have you made it this far? I hope that you have because this is now the final function of Dialectical Behavior Therapy. That function is to enhance the therapist's capabilities and support their motivation. DBT therapists work in a team to more effectively enhance the lives and understanding of their clients. This is important for the team as well as the client. A typical DBT team meeting may start with a mindfulness exercise, reading of the previous minutes, and then discuss strategies to further their treatment. It is important for you to be engaging and helpful along with your therapist as this whole treatment only works with your commitment. An example of this would be to imagine you and your therapist on a rowboat. Your therapist will not be able to motivate you to continue to row if they are not participating in the work. Your therapist can also not row by themselves if you are not helping. This whole style of treatment is designed to be a cooperative endeavor. You should feel excited and encouraged to participate. The end result will be a happier, more positive you!

This chapter is here to serve the purpose of relating what you have learned to the structured skills that are discussed in an actual Dialectical Behavior Therapy session. It is strongly encouraged that you attend these sessions and take what you have learned in this book with you to those sessions. There is nothing that you should not be able to achieve in this aspect of your life between this book, those sessions, and your own motivation! You have a threefold angle of attack on your negative habits that you wish to eradicate from your life. Finding a DBT session is easy, as it is a growing style of treatment. Everyone involved wishes only the best of success for you! Continue on with your own choices and feel proud of how far you have come!

Conclusion

Self-Compassion takes practice no doubt. One of the first few things you can do is to change the way you perceive self-compassion- by dispelling the myths and creating a positive perception towards self-love. Through the power of affirmations, creative visualization as well as changing your ideas of faith and believe, you can definitely start being more mindful of who you are what, and not based on your achievements and failures.

Knowing the myths of self-compassion is definitely one of the first things you should understand if you are really serious about wanting to be self-compassionate. This is only because whenever you feel like you are going to the downward spiral of thinking negative thoughts, you can always remember what self-compassion is and what self-compassion is not.

Self-compassion is a a good thing- keep this in mind so work on it because it does make you a better person.

You have truly made a huge impact on yourself, and quite possibly the biggest positive impact that you have made thus far in this journey of life. As I have said in the introduction, this was a journey made by your own choices. The secret about adventures is that they are never really over, and it is the journey, not the destination, that is the most exciting.

By the end of this book, you should have developed positive skills to replace your negative habits. Then you have applied those skills to your life in the form of practicing mindfulness, meditation, and Emotional Regulation. Then, you took it one step further and examined your life as it is now and developed the motivation to pursue social activities that reinforce your new positive life. This is a major victory for yourself and you should feel so proud of where you were, where you are now, and where you are most likely headed!

Like I have mentioned, it is strongly recommended to continue on in a DBT session. They are designed to work alongside you so that you do not have to put the progress that you have made on hold. The sessions usually take about a year to complete, but it will not be interfering with your life. This is your life at your own pace. You are most likely breathing easier, living better, and most importantly, feeling much more positive about you, your lifestyle, and your choices. Your family, peers, and colleagues are most likely excited to have the real you back, and it is now possible to continue on living without the weight of negative thought processes holding you back.

"With the new day comes new strength and new thoughts."

- Eleanor Roosevelt

I hope that this book has been a successful companion to you in your journey to discover the real you. Remember that this is not someone else's life that you are living. These are not processes designed to make you feel a certain, exact conclusion, but to merely enhance what it is about you that makes you the real you. Everyone has a positive side to them, everyone has a reason to celebrate themselves. Now, you are able to do so without the added pressure of negative thought processes, negative emotions, and negative habits. Go out and share your new self with the world. You are ready to become the best version of yourself!

www.ingramcontent.com/pod-product-compliance
Lightning Source LLC
Chambersburg PA
CBHW071406080526
44587CB00017B/3188